A Photo Gallery

# TROLLEY BUSES
# Around The World

## William A. Luke and Linda L. Metler

## Iconografix

**Iconografix**
PO Box 446
Hudson, Wisconsin 54016 USA

Library of Congress Control Number: 2006926932

ISBN-13: 978-1-58388-175-0
ISBN-10: 1-58388-175-1

06 07 08 09 10 11 6 5 4 3 2 1

Printed in China

Cover and book design by Dan Perry

Copyedited by Suzie Helberg

**On the cover:** main image- see page 31. Top, left to right- pages 62, 19, 72.

---

# Book Proposals

Iconografix is a publishing company specializing in books for transportation enthusiasts. We publish in a number of different areas, including Automobiles, Auto Racing, Buses, Construction Equipment, Emergency Equipment, Farming Equipment, Railroads & Trucks. The Iconografix imprint is constantly growing and expanding into new subject areas.

Authors, editors, and knowledgeable enthusiasts in the field of transportation history are invited to contact the Editorial Department at Iconografix, Inc., PO Box 446, Hudson, WI 54016.

# Table of Contents

# About the Authors

This is the third book on the history of bus transportation co-authored by William A. (Bill) Luke and Linda Metler. Both Bill and Linda have had many years of experience in writing articles and books about the bus industry. This book focuses on world trolley buses.

Bill began his bus industry career in 1948 with Jefferson Transportation Company at its general office in Minneapolis, Minnesota. Later he joined Empire Lines in Spokane, Washington.

In 1965, Bill and his wife, Adelene, began publishing the bus industry trade journal, *Bus Ride*.

Bill and Adelene's publishing venture was incorporated as Friendship Publications, Inc. As the editor and publisher of *Bus Ride*, Bill guided it to be an important source of information for the entire bus industry for more than 30 years. The company was sold in 1996.

Bill acquired an interest in bus transportation at an early age. Trolley buses had a special fascination and over the years Bill has photographed trolley buses in more than 25 countries. His first trolley bus picture was taken in Bern, Switzerland, in 1945 (see page 66). In addition to his own photographs, Bill has collected many other pictures and information from transit systems and friends worldwide.

In recent years Bill has done considerable traveling and writing. He has authored or co-authored 16 books on bus transportation history, beginning with the *Bus Industry Chronicle*, in 2000. He has traveled in all the states in the United States as well as all the Canadian provinces and has visited 70 other countries. He is the Executive Director of the Buses International Association, which he founded in 1981. Bill and Adelene continue to live in Spokane.

Linda became an employee of Friendship Publications as graphics manager and helped transition the company to desktop publishing. While with *Bus Ride*, she traveled extensively throughout the United States and Canada, visiting bus companies and transit agencies and conducting interviews of key people. Following the visits she wrote many articles for publication. These articles were often illustrated with pictures from her camera.

Linda and her husband, Don, a land surveyor, also live in Spokane. They have two grown daughters and three grandchildren.

# Acknowledgements

John Banks, Romiley, Stockport, United Kingdom
Andrea Baumann, Carroseria Hess, Bellach, Switzerland
Peter Blears, Horton, Illminster, United Kingdom
Danny Chan, Creative Master Northcord, Ltd., Hong Kong, China
Malcolm Chase, Fleet, Hants, United Kingdom
Ian Cooper, Canberra, Australia
Yves Goffin, Van Hool, Koningshooikt, Belgium
O. Iskov, Roskilde, Denmark
Doug Jack, Transport Resources International, Ashby St. Ledgers, United Kingdom
Stawomir Jarzabkowski, Solaris Bus & Coach, Owinska, Poland
D. A. Jones, London Trolley Bus Preservation Society, Gidea Park, United Kingdom
Tom Jones, Motor Bus Society, Clark, New Jersey, United States
Petr Kasencak, Skoda Electric, Pilsen, Czech Republic
Werner Kutil, TCAR/Veolia Transportation, Rouen, France
Loring Lawrence, Manchester, New Hampshire, United States
Paul Leger, Buses International Association, Halifax, Nova Scotia, Canada
Peter Maass, Vossloh Kiepe Corp., Ottawa, Ontario, Canada
Bill MacDonald, Victoria, British Columbia, Canada
Gunter Mackinger, Stad Salzburg, Salzburg, Austria
Gustavo A. Marqueta-Siibert Larrayad, Hispano Carrocera, SA, Zaragoza, Spain
Allen Morrison, New York City, New York, United States
Herb Pence, Manchester, New Hampshire, United States
Nikoley Petrakiev, Bulgaria
Wilhelm Pflug, Schuttorf, Germany
Alex Regiec, Winnipeg Transit, Winnipeg, Manitoba, Canada
Anton Reinbacher, Koflach, Austria
Cliff Scholes, Cincinnati, Ohio, United States
Brian Swinden, New Flyer Industries, Winnipeg, Manitoba, Canada
Nicolas Tellier, Irisbus, Chateaufort, France
Bohdan Turzanski, Lublin, Poland
Frank van der Boogert, Veteraan Autobussen Stichting, Leidschendam, Netherlands
Yukio Wada, Porte Publishing Co., Tokyo, Japan
Wisconsin Public Service Co.
Luc Wolters, Van Hool, Koningshooikt, Belgium

# Bibliography

**Books**

*50 Jahre Obus in Salzburg,* Austria

*50 Jahre Obus in Solingen* Christian Walther, Germany

*50 Let trolejbusove Dopravy v Pardubicich* Czech Republic

*50 Let Trolejbusu v Ostrava* Czech Republic

*Atlas trolejbusu* Ladislav Holub, Petr Vychodil, Juri Cermak, Czechoslovakia *Autobusy a trolejbusy Prague*
Czech Republic

*Bieler Strassenbahnen* Albert Ziegler, Claude Jeannaire, Switzerland

*Bournemouth Trolleybuses* Malcolm N. Pearce, United Kingdom

*British Trolleybuses in Colour* Kevin McCormick, United Kingdom

*BV Bus and Tram in the Czech Republic* Martin Harak, Czech Republic

*Cardiff Trolleybuses* Stephen Lockwood, United Kingdom

*Complete Encyclopedia of Commercial Vehicles* ,G. N. Georgano, United States

*Czech & Slovak Trolleybus & Tram Guide* ,Martin Harak, Czech Republic

*Double-Deck Trolleybuses of the World Beyond the British Isles* Brian Patton, United Kingdom

*Empire of the Trolleybus* Sergei Tarkhov, Russia

*Giro d'Italia in filobus* Paulo Gregorie, Francesco Rizzoli, Claudio Serra, France

*Histoire des Transports Jans les Villes de France* Jean Robert, France

*Les Trolleybus a Lyon* Jacques Perenon, Robert Chappelet, Rene Clevaud, France

*Les Trolleybus Francais* Rene Courant, Pascal Bejui, France

*London Bus & Tram Album* V. H. Darling, United Kingdom

*Obus in Osterreich* Gunter Mackinger, Austria

*Obus-Anlagen in Deutschland* Werner Stock, Germany

*Provos trolejbusu ve Zline a Otrokovicich*

*Round Europe by Trolleybus* Mike Russell, United Kingdom

*Round the World by Trolleybus* Alan Murray, United Kingdom

*Strassenbahnatlas 2004 Romanien*

*The Leyland Bus* D. Jack, United Kingdom

*Tradbuss Landskrona* Per Gunnar Andersson, Thomas Johansson

*Tradbussen i Svergie Del II* Leif Stolt, Sweden

*Tradbussen i Sverige Del I* Leif Stolt, Sweden

*Transit's Stepchild - The Trolley Coach* Mac Sebree, Paul Ward, United States

*Trolejbusy v Brne* Czech Republic

*Trolejbusy v Prazskych Ulicich* Jan Arazim, Miroslav Dyk, Jindrich Sour

*Trolley Buses 1913-2001 Photo Archive* William A. Luke, United States

*Trolleybus Trails* J. Joyce, United Kingdom

*Trolleybuses of Tasmania* I. G. Cooper, Australia

*Trolleybussene I Norge* Nils Carl Aspenberg, Norway

*Warszawski autobusy trolejbusy* Julian Dabrowski, Daniel Nalazek, Marcin Stiasny

*World Trolleybus Encyclopaedia* Alan Murray, United Kingdom

*World Trolleybus Pictorial* Alan Murray, United Kingdom

**Periodicals**

*Bus Industry Directory* various issues

*Bus Ride* Magazine various issues

*Jane's Urban Transport Systems*

*The Little Red Book 2000*

*Maly Atlas mestke dopravy 2002*

*McGraw Transit Directory* 1937

*Metropolitan Transportation Directory* 1962

*Metropolitan Transportation Directory* 1965

*Passenger Transport Yearbook 1963*

*Trolleybus* Magazine various issues

**In addition**

Newsletters, clippings, various Internet sites, and various publications of bus companies, transit agencies, and bus manufacturers

Interviews with bus-industry people from 1942-2006

# Foreword

This book has been an interesting project, not only for its subject matter, the trolley bus, but also for the challenges involved in gathering the information. In attempting to include as many past and present trolley bus systems as possible, a tremendous amount of research was required. This involved reviewing many publications in languages other than English, the only language the authors speak (although many words in different languages have become familiar). A further complication came from the fact that many of the companies, organizations, or manufacturers building or operating trolley buses have changed their names over the years, and many are no longer in business.

We have attempted to acquire the best information possible from a variety of sources. However, the sources did not always agree on historical facts, company names, the spelling of names and words, or, it seems, just about anything else. We apologize in advance for any errors that have been made. We did the best we could.

Of the more than 325 trolley bus pictures in the book, approximately one-third came from trolley bus historians, manufacturers, and operating systems around the world that were contacted. One-third of the pictures came from William A. Luke's extensive collection of photographs, many of which have come from trolley bus historians, manufacturers, and operators during the past 40 to 50 years. The final one-third came from photographs taken by William Luke, himself.

We have tried to include as much information as possible about each of the trolley buses that are pictured. Many of our sources did not include information about the makers of the chassis, motors, electric components, and other important features of each trolley bus. Therefore, in most cases, we have not included chassis and motor/electrics information.

Some of the photographs in our files did not properly identify the trolley bus. Sometimes the trolley bus could be identified by its number. In one case, a trolley bus was identified by the route name on its destination board.

We used our best judgment in dealing with language differences and political changes. One example is the use of English versions of city names. For the sake of clarity, if not political correctness, in most cases we have chosen to use the English version of capital cities; for instance, Rome rather than Roma, and Copenhagen rather than Kobenhavns, but have used the local language version for most other cities. When we felt there would be confusion, we used the English version with the local language version in parentheses or vise versa.

At the back of the book there is an Index of all the operating systems and manufacturers of trolley buses mentioned in the book. As we were compiling information, we wished that the books we used for research had included such an index; it would have made the job much easier. We hope that people searching for trolley bus information from our book will be able to find it easily.

Following the Index is another alphabetical index of the cities mentioned in the book that operated trolley bus systems today or have operated them in the past.

Several directories were used in researching this book, along with many other publications. One particular book, *The World Trolley Bus Encyclopaedia,* by Alan Murray of the United Kingdom, was an especially useful resource. *Trolleybus* Magazine, a regular periodical published in the United Kingdom, has also been valuable for research. All the books and other materials used are listed in the Bibliography. Many individuals throughout the world were very helpful in furnishing pictures, information, and translations, and they are listed in the Acknowledgements.

In any of the bus transportation books we have authored, a bit of trivia has always added interest, and this book has followed that pattern. As we worked on this manuscript, we learned much about trolley buses, the countries and cities of the world, and the changes that have been taking place around the globe. It is our hope that the many trolley bus historians, enthusiasts, and others who read this book will enjoy it and find it useful.

# Introduction

For more than a century trolley buses have been providing transportation in towns and cities throughout the world. One of the earliest types of motorized transportation, the trolley bus has been known by a number of names, including trolley bus, trolleybus, trolley coach, trackless trolley, rail-less car, rail-less tram, and, most recently, electric trolley bus or ETB. But no matter what name is used the trolley bus is easily recognized by its most distinctive feature, a pair of poles mounted on the roof. These poles provide electric power to the trolley bus through contact with overhead wires, like a street car. But unlike a street car the trolley bus runs on rubber tires.

Trolley bus development began in Europe in the late 1800s. Although the trolley bus enjoyed a fair amount of success during those first experimental years, most of the early installations were small and short-lived. The trolley bus was utilitarian. Not as glamorous as a street car or as modern as the motor bus, it never received the same attention as those other modes of transportation. However, the trolley bus offered several advantages over other vehicles, including quiet operation, quick acceleration from a standing start, and a long life span. The hill-climbing ability of trolley buses was another distinct advantage, and a number of hilly cities favored the trolley bus and continue to do so.

The trolley bus receives its power through a positively charged overhead wire. The current is fed through electrical control equipment to a motor or motors on the vehicle and returned through a second, negatively charged, overhead wire. The poles on the trolley bus make contact with the wires and are fitted with springs on the roof to provide tension to keep the ends of the poles in contact with the running wires. During winter snowstorms overhead wires can sometimes become clogged with ice, disrupting the operation of the trolley bus. There have been occasions when regular motor buses have been equipped with trolley poles to scrape ice off the wires in order to allow the trolley buses to operate under electrical power.

How electric current was supplied to the trolley bus varied in the first years, with different countries developing different systems for use on their trolley buses. Various voltages, different ways of placing the poles on the vehicles (side by side, on top of one another, and at various widths), and various methods of return-ing the poles into contact with the wires following a "dewiring" were utilized. However, after 1930 virtually all trolley buses were operated with two separated poles on top connected to two wires. Some systems using dual-powered vehicles have modern methods to remove the poles from the wire when converting to auxiliary power.

Different systems for changing the direction the trolley bus was traveling along the wires were also developed, including a turnaround at the end of the route, or, rarely, a turntable at the end of the route. A double-ended trolley bus was even produced in the early 1900s, but the idea was not pursued until much later with a system in Seraing, Belgium.

Initially, the trolley bus was of interest primarily to street car companies or tram systems wishing to utilize their investment in electric power and distribution systems. Trolley buses were seen as a way of making use of a proven power source without the considerable startup costs associated with street car systems. Until 1918 almost all trolley bus systems consisted of a few vehicles on a single route, sometimes as a feeder for a street car route, or a replacement for a street car route. Just a few of these early systems survived after World War I.

The first trolley buses were strongly influenced by the design of the street car. As trolley bus technology improved in the 1920s, several towns found the trolley bus to be a good choice for their operations. By 1930 the trolley bus had evolved, taking on many designs and components of the motor bus, and the trolley bus became an important vehicle for city transportation. Modern trolley buses emerged in many European countries although few really large systems were created. Many manufacturers of trolley buses also built motor buses, utilizing the same bodywork.

During World War II fuel oil was scarce, and cities were encouraged to introduce new trolley bus systems or expand existing ones. Austria, France, Germany, Italy, Spain, and Switzerland all opened new trolley bus systems. The typical wartime trolley bus system was relatively small, sometimes just a single route with a handful of vehicles.

The 15 years following World War II were peak years for the trolley bus. Existing street car and tram lines had experienced hard use during the war. Replacing a street car or tram system was often very expensive, not only in the cost of the track, but also in the vehicles themselves. Trolley bus systems were less expensive and were felt to be a good option for many cities. A number of new systems were started, especially in Europe.

Several factors contributed to the elimination of some trolley bus systems in the years following World War II and to the gradual decrease in trolley bus growth in the 1950s and 1960s. Although many European trolley bus systems were small, cities felt the need to reduce the number of different kinds of transportation vehicles. In addition, new infrastructure and vehicles were needed. And the price of electricity had risen faster than fuel oil prices, making the use of home-produced power supplies less economical. The motor bus, being cheaper to run and more flexible, gained in popularity.

Trolley bus manufacturing became very important in the years immediately following World War II. European manufacturers, notably in Italy, France, and Germany, were supplying new trolley bus markets in South America, Africa, and other parts of the world. The United Kingdom not only supplied vehicles for its own systems, but also for many countries in the British Commonwealth and elsewhere. Manufacturers in the United States were busy meeting the needs of U.S. trolley bus systems, but also produced exports to other countries, particularly in South America and Turkey.

Throughout the history of the trolley bus, larger vehicles were developed to increase the number of passengers that could be carried. Both two-axle and three-axle trolley buses had a period of popularity, with the three-axle providing a stable, comfortable ride and room for nearly as many passengers as a street car or tram. London Transport developed the three-axle, double-deck trolley bus, and had a large number in its fleet. Double-deck trolley buses also appeared in other countries. Trolley buses in some countries in the early days were operated with passenger trailers to increase their passenger-carrying capabilities.

The first articulated trolley buses appeared in the 1930s. They were reportedly built in Italy and used in Milan. It was not until later in the century that the use of articulated trolley buses accelerated. In the United States only one articulated trolley bus was built prior to 1946, and no other articulated trolley buses were built in the United States or Canada until late in the twentieth century.

The earliest trolley buses required two motors to provide the power necessary to perform their jobs, but a single 125-horsepower motor became standard in the mid-1930s. As larger trolley buses were introduced after World War II, 140-horsepower motors were often employed. Though they were much more powerful, they were still lightweight. The use of aluminum played an important role in reducing the weight, yet enhancing the strength of the trolley bus, making operations more economical. Another very important technology, and a very important advantage for trolley buses, was dynamic braking. Mechanical air brakes wore out rapidly and using the motor for breaking was desirable for trolley buses.

Dual-mode trolley buses, which run on electricity but also have auxiliary engines, have appeared from time to time and have even larger diesel engines, as much as 280 horsepower. There have also been some trolley buses with auxiliary power from batteries stored on the vehicles. The use of dual-mode trolley buses allowed systems to operate extensions into outlying areas without the expense of providing wire and power. Trolley buses could operate on diesel power in those areas, but could run under electrical power when they returned to the city. This was greatly favored by environmentalists. In addition, dual-mode trolley buses could be diverted around construction sites where it was not appropriate to add new trolley bus wires over detoured routes.

The largest operator of dual-mode trolley buses was an early installation for the Public Service Coordinated Transport Company of New Jersey, which began using dual-mode trolley buses in 1935. More than 500 gas/electric trolley buses were placed in service on 22 routes in the urban areas of Newark and Camden, but the system lasted just 13 years.

The new trolley bus system in Rome, Italy, operates on batteries in the city center to avoid having overhead wires in the environmentally sensitive city center. In Quito, Ecuador, the trolley bus maintenance facility has no wires. The dual-mode trolley buses used in Quito reach the maintenance facility under electrical power but then are moved around the maintenance site on diesel power.

In the 1980s dual-mode trolley buses reappeared in several countries. Notable examples include systems in Nancy, France; Essen, Germany; and Seattle, Washington. Seattle has a very narrow central business district that contributes to considerable traffic congestion.

In 1990 the city built a 1.3-mile-long transit tunnel under the downtown area. Because of the length of the tunnel and the possible pollution that might be generated by diesel engines, it was decided that only electric trolley buses should be operated in the tunnel. Dual-mode trolley buses could emerge from the tunnel and operate on regular routes without overhead wiring. Today, with improvements in diesel engines and in hybrid technology, the use of trolley buses in the tunnel is not crucial. Newer buses can operate in the tunnel under electrical power from batteries. In addition, the new hybrid vehicles are very good at climbing hills, once a distinct advantage of the trolley bus over its diesel counterparts.

In addition to transporting passengers, trolley buses have also been used for other purposes, such as carrying freight. There have been more than 30 non-passenger trolley vehicle systems, mostly in the early 1900s and again in more recent years. Trolley buses have been used for underground mining operations, and an underground trolley bus system in Japan carries sightseers through a tunnel to a recently constructed hydroelectric dam.

Longevity is a characteristic of the trolley bus. Life spans of fifty years are not uncommon, and thirty years has been achieved by hundreds of trolley buses. Given proper preventive maintenance, the trolley bus can remain in operation longer than the motor bus, thanks, in part, to the lack of bodywork vibrations and wear-and-tear caused by the internal combustion engine. In Valparaiso, Chile, Pullman-Standard trolley buses built in the United States and delivered in the late 1940s are still in operation. These are considered the oldest trolley buses still in regular service in the world today.

Despite their long life, or possibly because of it, the trolley bus sometimes has a public image as an old-fashioned, out-of-date mode of transportation. Motor buses have had many changes in design over the years, making them more attractive and more comfortable for the passengers. Older trolley buses, with their high-floor design, have become outdated. During World War II, in the United Kingdom and elsewhere, older chassis and electrical equipment were given new bodies. Rebodying could change a trolley bus from a single to a double deck and vice versa, and serviceable electrical equipment was also reused in other vehicles. This practice has been revived in recent years. In the Canadian cities of Toronto and Hamilton, Ontario, a number of trolley buses were rebodied, beginning in 1970, and in 2000 a fleet of 100 trolley buses were rebodied in Seattle, with bodies by Gillig Corporation and Alstrom motors taken from older AM General vehicles.

Ironically, the longevity of the trolley bus has contributed to its own undoing. With few large orders for replacement vehicles and few new systems, manufacturers made relatively few technical or design improvements, and trolley bus numbers declined with competition from other, more modern modes of transportation. The high cost and low flexibility of trolley bus systems also made other transportation modes more economical. However, the biggest competition for the trolley bus, in fact for public transportation of all kinds, has been the emergence of the private automobile.

During the 1950s and 1960s, many trolley bus systems were abandoned, including not only some small-size systems, but also larger systems such as those in London, Rome, Belfast, Prague, Stockholm, and Barcelona. Apart from Europe and North America, in the 1960s and 1970s the majority of systems in non-communist countries of the world closed. Exceptions included Johannesburg, South Africa, which continued operating its system until 1986, and Wellington, New Zealand, which still operates trolley buses today. In Brazil trolley bus service declined to some extent, but the domestic manufacturing industry continued to meet the needs for trolley bus replacements.

The oil crisis of the 1970s marked the end of the period of trolley bus system closures, and the number of trolley bus systems in the world has risen steadily, though not dramatically, since then. Ecological concerns have encouraged the continued use of trolley buses in many areas and the environmental movement has made it difficult to close existing trolley bus systems. Rome, Italy, has reintroduced trolley buses.

Although many trolley bus systems have ceased

operations in Western Europe, in Eastern Europe trolley bus systems have continued to be popular. Some of the largest systems now exist in Russia, Ukraine, Belarus, and other Eastern European countries. Trolley bus manufacturing in Eastern Europe has flourished. In Russia, the Uritsky Company (reportedly now known as the Trolza Company), which is known for its ZIU trolley buses, has been producing a record number of trolley buses, probably the most trolley buses ever manufactured. Not only has it supplied cities in Russia and others cities in the former Soviet Union, but many ZIU trolley buses have appeared in other countries in Eastern and Southern Europe and South America.

Another important trolley bus manufacturer in Eastern Europe is the electrical firm Skoda in the Czech Republic. In 2004 the Skoda plant in Ostrov, Czech Republic, was closed. Skoda Electrical Company has continued, however, focusing on the production of rail vehicles, and supplying motors for trolley buses to the Czech Republic and other Eastern European countries, including Ukraine. Skoda trolley buses have also appeared in Bergen, Norway, and other cities around the world. In recent years the company has supplied trolley buses to Kabul, Afghanistan, and Tehran, Iran, and in cooperation with the American firm AAI, a subsidiary of United Industrial Corp., Skoda trolley buses have also been delivered to systems in the United States, including Dayton, Ohio, and San Francisco, California.

The Czech bus builder Karosa is now building the trolley bus bodies that were originally built at the Ostrov plant. A newly merged company, Irisbus, which includes Renault, the French bus builder, and other manufacturers in Italy and Spain, has acquired an interest in Karosa. Skoda trolley buses are now being built with bodies from Irisbus at the former Renault plant in France. At present, Irisbus is mainly supplying ultramodern Cristalis trolley buses to systems in France.

Another important European trolley bus manufacturer, Solaris Bus & Coach, had never built a trolley bus prior to 2002, but since then has become an important trolley bus manufacturer. Located in Poland, Solaris has supplied new trolley buses to a number of cities in its own area plus a number of vehicles to the new system in Rome, Italy, a small system in Landskrona, Sweden, and to several cities in Switzerland.

Ikarus, which has been a major builder of motor buses in Hungary, has supplied trolley buses for many cities in Eastern Europe and elsewhere in recent years. Its original body design was drastically changed in the 1990s and a new trolley bus design was introduced. This is particularly noted in the system in Budapest, Hungary.

New Flyer Industries in Winnipeg, Manitoba, Canada, is one of the most important bus manufacturers in North America. New Flyer has received a big order for new low-floor and standard and articulated trolley buses from Vancouver, British Columbia.

Hispano Carrocera, a company in Spain, has supplied all the new trolley bus bodies for the trolley bus system in Quito, Ecuador, and has received a new order for trolley buses in Merida, Venezuela, a system that has not begun operations, although the trolley buses have been delivered.

Italian builders are also active in building trolley buses, along with the Belgian manufacturer Van Hool, and the Dutch manufacturer Berkhof. The German manufacturer MAN, now known as Neoman, is also building new trolley buses. In the United States no new trolley buses are being built, although the Gillig Corporation has supplied the bodies for rebuilt trolley buses in Seattle.

In today's world, transit systems are seldom operated by private companies, but more often by local and regional governments. As a result, politics enters into many transportation decisions. Throughout its history, the fate of the trolley bus has had as much to do with political concerns and public opinion as with the vehicles themselves, and that continues to this day. The growth of bus rapid transit systems and newer developments in diesel engine and hybrid technology for buses, along with the desire to eliminate overhead wiring in city streets, has slowed the development of trolley buses in the western world, particularly in South America. Volatile political concerns in some areas have affected the growth or continuance of trolley bus systems.

The Merrill (Wisconsin) Railway & Lighting Company was one of the first companies to operate a commercial trolley bus service in a U.S. city. The first trolley bus in Merrill, which is shown here, was the only one built by Field Electric Bus Co. It had hard rubber tires and an interesting chain drive. The Merrill trolley bus line began in 1913 and was discontinued in 1919. *Wisconsin Public Service Co.*

# North America

### United States

Most of the early trolley bus systems in the United States were experimental and did not last long. One early example was a system for real estate promoters in Laurel Canyon in California. One of the first trolley bus lines built by an established transportation company was in Merrill, Wisconsin, in 1913.

The J. G. Brill Company of Philadelphia introduced the first standardized production model trolley bus in the United States, the Brill "Rail-less" car, in 1922. There were several other early manufacturers who built trolley buses, but most produced only a few vehicles and did not become longtime trolley bus builders.

Philadelphia began operating 29-passenger Rail-less

cars on Orange Avenue in 1923. This was the first permanent trolley bus system in the United States and has lasted into the 21st Century. There were a few other early systems, including: Baltimore, Maryland, which operated a first trolley bus system from 1922 to 1931; Cohoes, New York, which had a trolley bus system between 1924 and 1937; and Rochester, New York, which had a similar operation from 1923 to 1932. In addition, systems began in Salt Lake City, Utah, in 1928 and in New Orleans, Louisiana, in 1929. These two systems lasted until after World War II.

Beginning in the 1930s a number of manufacturers began producing trolley buses in large numbers. In fact, nearly all transit vehicle manufacturers branched into building trolley buses. Some of these were companies that built motor buses, but there were also some, like the Pullman-Standard Company and St. Louis Car Company, which were dominant street car builders. Of the major trolley bus builders, only the Marmon-Herrington Company was not already well known for its transit vehicles when it began producing trolley buses in 1946. The Twin Coach Company, a pioneer in motor bus development, Yellow Coach (General Motors), and Mack Trucks were also dominant in the trolley bus manufacturing field. The General Electric Co. and Westinghouse were the main suppliers of motors and electrics in trolley buses in the United States.

ACF-Brill and Pullman-Standard Company were the largest producers of trolley buses in the United States, both building almost 2,000 trolley buses. Although the St. Louis Car Company produced four trolley buses prior to 1930, its main production began in 1930 and continued until 1951, with more than 1,100 trolley buses produced. The Twin Coach

Petersburg, Virginia, operated a small trolley bus operation between 1923 and 1928. There were two J. G. Brill trolley buses in service, one of which is pictured here. The J. G. Brill Company built 21 of these vehicles, which were called Rail-less Cars. Similar Rail-less Cars operated in Los Angeles, Baltimore, and Philadelphia. The Petersburg system was operated by the Virginia Railway & Power Co., which also experimented with trolley buses in the early 1920s in Richmond and Norfolk, Virginia. *Herb Pence*

The Utah Light and Traction Company in Salt Lake City began trolley bus operations in 1928, but closed in 1946. The first Salt Lake City trolley bus was a Model 40 Twin Coach, the first trolley bus built by the Twin Coach Company. Twin Coach built 658 trolley buses in 21 years. Pictured is one of the eight Twin Coach trolley buses that were in service in Salt Lake City. The Versare or Cincinnati companies built the remainder of the Salt Lake City trolley buses. *Motor Bus Society*

The Yellow Truck & Coach Manufacturing Co., a division of General Motors in Pontiac, Michigan, built its first trolley buses in 1932. These first 12 trolley buses, models 701-MT-A, were sold to the Wisconsin Gas & Electric Co. for its operation in Kenosha, Wisconsin. These were joined by 10 trolley buses built by the St. Louis Car Co. For a time, only trolley buses were used for urban transit in Kenosha. The trolley bus service in Kenosha ended in 1952.

Company started building trolley buses in 1928 and built 658 trolley buses through 1949. Yellow Coach Company built 456 trolley buses from 1932 through 1938, including some 356 All Service Vehicles that were powered both by gasoline engines and electrical power and operated in New Jersey.

Mack built 290 trolley buses between 1934 and 1943 before discontinuing trolley bus manufacturing after World War II. The Marmon-Herrington Company built 1,513 trolley buses before completing its last order in 1955. There were several other smaller builders of trolley buses in the United States, but since 1972, most trolley bus manufacturing for the United States has been done by Flyer Industries of Winnipeg, Canada, now known as New Flyer Industries.

The development of large-capacity (40 seats or more) trolley buses helped the trolley bus compete with street cars. However, in the early 1930s most trolley bus systems were feeder lines for a city rail system. From an economic standpoint, the Great Depression probably helped the trolley bus take a foothold in a few cities that would otherwise have gone directly from rail to gasoline buses. In the early 1930s a number of large cities in the United States established extensive trolley bus systems, including Chicago, which placed 74 trolley buses into service in 1930, more units than had been built or operated in the entire history of the trolley bus up to that time.

In the 1930s and 1940s some smaller cities also began replacing street car lines with trolley buses. For instance: St. Joseph, Missouri, began trolley bus service in 1932; Duluth, Minnesota, started in 1931; Greenville, South Carolina, in 1934; and Kenosha, Wisconsin, in 1932. The Kenosha system, which lasted until 1952, was unusual. The 22 trolley buses operated there were the only transit vehicles to operate in that city. All other cities had supplementary transportation systems with street cars and/or motor buses.

Sixty-seven different systems operated over the years in the United States, but by the late 1960s only five systems remained. They were in Seattle, San Francisco, Boston, Philadelphia, and Dayton, Ohio. Environmental concerns have contributed to the retention of these last five systems, which now operate trolley buses built by several different manufacturers, including some imported models.

The Brooklyn (New York) Bus Company began operating trolley buses in 1930. There were four trolley buses in the early fleet, one ACF, two Twin Coaches, and one Osgood Bradley. Six Pullman-Standard trolley buses were added in 1932. The New York City Board of Transportation acquired the Brooklyn Bus Company in 1940. In 1948, streetcar lines in Brooklyn were being converted to trolley buses and this led to the purchase of 200 St. Louis Car Co. trolley buses. One is pictured. That was the second-largest purchase of trolley buses up until that time in the United States. Trolley bus service continued in Brooklyn until 1960. *Motor Bus Society*

The Boston (Massachusetts) Elevated Railway is celebrating 70 years of continuous trolley bus service. Pullman-Standard trolley buses were the choice for vehicles in Boston. From the beginning of the system until 1945 the Boston service acquired 157 Pullman-Standard trolley buses. Pictured is one of the 40-passenger models added in 1937. Pullman-Standard Car Manufacturing Corp. in Chicago began building railway-sleeping cars in 1867. Its first streetcars were built in 1891. When the company acquired the Osgood Bradley Company in Worcester, Massachusetts, trolley bus production began. Pullman-Standard was responsible for 1,906 trolley buses between 1932 and 1951. Boston received the last 90 built.

Dayton, a smaller United States city, has imported trolley buses that originated in the Czech Republic. San Francisco also acquired both standard and articulated trolley buses from the Czech Republic. Beginning in 1988, Seattle purchased a fleet of 236 Breda dual-mode vehicles from Italy for use in its downtown tunnel.

The United States, unlike many other countries, did not export very many of its trolley buses. One of the few pre-World War II examples was the exportation of 56 trolley buses to the system in Ankara, Turkey. Several cities in South America also acquired trolley buses built in the United States. After the closing of many trolley bus systems in the United States some of the used trolley buses were exported to Mexico.

In recent years dual-mode trolley buses have become common in a number of cities. However, between 1935 and 1948 there were 356 dual-powered trolley buses operated by the Public Service Coordinated Transport in New Jersey. These trolley buses, more appropriately called All Service Vehicles (ASV), operated routes in the Newark and Camden areas. The Yellow Truck & Coach Manufacturing Co. built them. The ASVs traveled on electrical power in urban areas and gasoline engines were used in outlying areas.

Denver (Colorado) Tramway Corp. began replacing some street car lines with trolley buses in 1940. The initial fleet consisted of 45 Brill Model 44SMT trolley buses. Seventeen more, including the one pictured, were acquired in 1941 and 1942. The fleet of Denver trolley buses continued to expand but the service ended in 1955. At its peak, Denver had about 200 trolley buses.

Cleveland (Ohio) Railway Company began trolley bus service in 1936 and continued until 1963. The first trolley buses operating in Cleveland were built by the St. Louis Car Co. Only one Twin Coach trolley bus operated in Cleveland and it was unusual for its time. The one-of-a-kind vehicle was an articulated trolley bus built in 1940 and called the Super Twin. The articulation was only in a vertical direction and it had a steerable rear axle. This trolley bus served until 1954. Cleveland had a very large trolley bus fleet. *Motor Bus Society*

The Twin Coach Company of Kent, Ohio, was one of seven major builders of trolley buses in the United States. The first Twin Coach trolley bus was built in 1928 and operated in Salt Lake City. Chicago received 58 Twin Coach trolley buses in 1930/31. The largest order for Twin Coach trolley buses came from the Seattle (Washington) Transit System in 1940. One of the 135 trolley buses that entered Seattle service at that time is pictured. In 1942, 18 more Twin Coach trolley buses were acquired, followed by 24 in 1943. At the time Seattle had one of the largest trolley bus fleets in the United States. Trolley buses were especially efficient on Seattle's steep hills. Seattle continues to operate a large trolley bus fleet.

The Yellow Truck & Coach Manufacturing Co., of Pontiac, Michigan, built a total of 456 trolley buses. However, only 100 were built as pure trolley buses; the other 356 were All Service Vehicles. The Milwaukee Electric Railway and Light Company (TMER) had 40 Yellow Coach trolley buses, one of which is pictured here. TMER began trolley bus service in 1936 and continued for almost 30 years. It was a very large trolley bus system with 419 vehicles at the peak. A variety of trolley buses were operated in Milwaukee, including vehicles built by Twin Coach, St. Louis Car Co., Pullman-Standard, and Marmon-Herrington.

In 1945 the Dallas (Texas) Railway & Terminal Company acquired 30 ACF-Brill Model TC44 trolley buses to inaugurate trolley bus service in the city. Another 24 of the same model were delivered soon afterward. Dallas also had sixteen 1952 Marmon-Herrington trolley buses in its fleet. Air conditioning for trolley buses was not available as a standard at that time, but Dallas added air conditioning. The unit can be seen on the top of this ACF-Brill trolley bus. Service with trolley buses in Dallas ended in 1966.

The trolley bus system in Ohio's capital, Columbus, was one of the earliest in the state, beginning in 1933. The Brill Company was the first to supply trolley buses to Columbus, with 85 acquired between 1933 and 1940. There were also 18 St. Louis Car Company trolley buses in the early fleet. Columbus added 138 Marmon-Herrington trolley buses in 1947-1948, one of which is pictured.

The Birmingham (Alabama) Electric Company didn't begin trolley bus service until 1947, and then it only lasted 11 years. The system had a large fleet of 148 Pullman-Standard trolley buses; in fact all Birmingham trolley buses were built by Pullman-Standard. The first order for trolley buses came in 1946 and went into service the next year. One of the 63 additional Pullman-Standard trolley buses purchased in 1947 is pictured here. Pullman-Standard built 1,906 trolley buses between 1922 and 1951.

The Twin Coach Company built its first trolley buses in 1928. Between then and 1949, 500 were built. In 1948 and 1949 a new modern design was introduced, but only 151 were built. Ninety of these were delivered to the San Francisco (California) Municipal Railway (Muni). One of Muni's Model 44TTW Twin Coach trolley buses is pictured. Muni began trolley bus service in 1935 and it continues to have an active fleet. The hilly terrain in San Francisco has been well suited to trolley bus operation.

St. Joseph, Missouri, was a small city in the United States that decided to begin a trolley bus system. It started replacement of street cars in 1932. Pictured is a 1947 ACF-Brill Model TC44 trolley bus that was originally in service by the Wilkes-Barre (Pennsylvania) Transit Corporation. It was acquired by the St. Joseph Railway Light Heat and Power Company in 1959 and operated until the system closed in 1966. American Car and Foundry Company (ACF) began in 1926 and joined with the Brill Company in 1945. Trolley buses and buses were built under the ACF-Brill name until 1952. Changes in the design of the trolley buses were made in 1947 and again in 1948.

New Orleans, Louisiana, was one of the first large U.S. cities to operate trolley buses. The New Orleans Public Service Company, Inc. (NOPSI) operated the service. It began in 1929 with a Model 513-1-H11 ACF Motors trolley bus. Eleven Cincinnati Car Co. vehicles followed the next year. New Orleans became partial to St. Louis Car Co. trolley buses and added 154 new ones in 1947 and 1948. However, NOPSI also had 49 Marmon-Herrington trolley buses, one of which is pictured here in the city's famous French Quarter. The trolley bus system in New Orleans ended in 1967.

The Georgia Power Co. in Atlanta operated one of the largest trolley bus fleets in the United States. The maximum number of trolley buses in service was 453. Trolley buses first came to Atlanta in 1937 and they operated until 1963. In 1949, 140 trolley buses of a new design built by the St. Louis Car Company were introduced in Atlanta. They had slanted sides, large side windows with sliding sash, aluminum side trim, and other features. These 140 trolley buses were the only ones in Atlanta built by the St. Louis Car Co. Most of the Atlanta trolley buses were built by the Pullman-Standard Company, including the first air-conditioned trolley bus in the world. Other air-conditioned trolley buses were considered at the time, but the technology was not yet reliable. Atlanta also had Brill and Twin Coach trolley buses in the 1930s and 1940s.

Chicago, Illinois, had the largest trolley bus system in the United States. It began under the Chicago Surface Lines in 1930 with 40 Model 40TT Twin Coach trolley buses. The system expanded, and a variety of trolley buses were acquired, including vehicles from Brill, Cincinnati Car, St. Louis Car, and Pullman-Standard. When the Chicago Transit Authority (CTA) acquired the Chicago Surface Lines in 1947, a trolley bus fleet renewal was underway. The largest purchase of trolley buses at one time came in 1951 when the CTA bought 349 trolley buses from the Marmon-Herrington Company. In 1937 there were 135 trolley buses in Chicago, and by 1962 there were 554. Trolley bus numbers began to decline in Chicago in the 1960s, and the service ended in 1973.

Johnstown (Pennsylvania) Traction Company featured several interesting trolley bus facts. It was the last trolley bus system established in the United States. That was in 1951. Of the modern systems it was relatively short lived, serving only 16 years, but it outlasted a number of systems in the country. Only six new trolley buses were purchased by the Johnstown Traction Company. They were all built by the St. Louis Car Company in 1951, and were among the last of the 1,119 trolley buses built by the company. One of the St. Louis Car Co. trolley buses is pictured in Johnstown.

The Marmon-Herrington Company, Indianapolis, Indiana, built 1,513 trolley buses in the eight years the company was in business. Its first trolley bus was built in 1946 and the last in 1955. The Kansas City (Missouri) Public Service, which began operating trolley buses in 1938, made a one-time purchase of 60 Marmon-Herrington trolley buses in 1947. One is pictured here. Trolley buses operated in Kansas City until early 1959. A total of 176 trolley buses had been acquired. In addition to the Marmon-Herringtons, there were also Macks, Twin Coaches, and Brills in Kansas City.

The Massachusetts Bay Transportation Authority (MBTA) of Boston acquired the Boston Elevated Railway in 1964. At that time there were 160 trolley buses in service. Times have changed and the fleet was reduced to 43 trolley buses, but service continues, mainly because of tunnel operations. In 1976, 50 trolley buses were purchased from Flyer Industries, one of which is pictured. These trolley buses had a left-side passenger door to facilitate unloading passengers in the subway stations in the tunnel. *Herb Pence*

The Philadelphia (Pennsylvania) Rapid Transit Company (PRT) first established trolley bus service on Philadelphia's Oregon Avenue in 1923. The system's first vehicles were eight Brill Rail-less Car trolley buses with hard rubber tires and wooden bodies. Brill was located in Philadelphia, and only Brill trolley buses were acquired until 1949, when 28 Marmon-Herrington trolley buses were added. In 1955 PRT bought the last 43 trolley buses built by Marmon-Herrington. It was necessary to renew the trolley bus fleet in Philadelphia in the 1970s, and in 1978 AM General trolley buses, one of which is pictured here, were acquired by the Southeastern Pennsylvania Transportation Authority, the transit operator at the time. Service had been suspended and the future of Philadelphia trolley buses was uncertain until a decision was made to continue service.

Dayton (Ohio) Street Railway Company began trolley bus service in 1933, after a fire destroyed many of its street cars. The first Dayton trolley buses were 12 Brill Model T-40 vehicles. There were four other transit systems in Dayton. The Oakwood Street Railway Co., Peoples Railway Company, and City Railway Company all began operating trolley buses in 1936. The Dayton-Xenia Railway Company began its trolley bus operation in 1941. The companies merged into the City Transit Company in 1955/56. Public ownership in Dayton came in 1972 with the formation of the Miami Valley Regional Transit Authority (MVRTA). In 1975, 64 of these new E800 Flyer Industries trolley buses replaced older ones in Dayton.

Breda Construzioni Ferrovierie in Italy supplied the Municipality of Metropolitan Seattle (Washington) with 236 dual-powered trolley buses in 1990. These vehicles were dual-powered so they could be used in Seattle's downtown transit tunnel, where only electric trolley buses operated. After leaving the tunnel, the trolley buses ran under diesel power to outlying areas of metropolitan Seattle. One of the Breda trolley buses is pictured here in the tunnel.

The Miami Valley Regional Transit Authority in Dayton, Ohio, took delivery of 57 new trolley buses in 1998 to replace older vehicles. Skoda Ostrov in the Czech Republic initiated the building of the trolley bus order. One of these trolley buses is pictured here. They were completed by AAI, a subsidiary of United Industrial Corporation, using the name Electric Transit, Inc., for the joint venture. Dayton's first trolley bus operator was the Dayton Street Railway Co., which began service in 1933.

San Francisco (California) Municipal Railway has been operating trolley buses since 1941. Renewal of the large trolley bus fleet has taken place a number of times, and in 1993, 60 New Flyer Model E60 trolley buses replaced older trolley buses. They were the first articulated trolley buses built by New Flyer Industries of Winnipeg, Manitoba. One of these trolley buses is pictured on Mission Street. San Francisco's fleet numbers more than 350 trolley buses, similar to the number of trolley buses in Seattle.

Pictured is one of the 100 trolley buses with bodies by the Gillig Corporation now operated in Seattle, Washington, by the King County Department of Transportation. These 100 trolley buses have refurbished motors that came from the 1979 AM General trolley buses that were replaced. The new trolley buses began appearing on Seattle streets in 2001. Alstrom Transportation Company successfully refurbished the motors.

In 2001 San Francisco (California) Municipal Railway (Muni) began replacing older trolley buses with 250 units from the Czech Republic firm, Skoda and its U.S. partner AAI/ETI. Of the 250 trolley buses, 38 are articulated and 220 are standard trolley buses. They are all high-floor models. Trolley bus service by Muni began in 1941, although the Market Street Railway in San Francisco began a nine-vehicle trolley bus operation in 1935. It was eventually acquired by Muni.

Massachusetts Bay Transportation Authority (MBTA) in Boston inaugurated a new Bus Rapid Transit service, the Silver Line, in 2002. A fleet of 32 new silver articulated Neoplan duo buses were acquired at that time. The service is being extended in several stages and will be completed in 2009. The Silver Line travels through an underground transitway between the South Station and Boston's Logan Airport. While in the tunnel the vehicles operate as trolley buses, otherwise a diesel engine is used. One of the Silver Line trolley buses is pictured. *Herb Pence*

The Massachusetts Bay Transportation Authority (MBTA), along with its predecessor company, has been operating trolley buses in Boston since 1936. As the 21st Century began it was decided to replace the aging fleet of almost 30-year-old Flyer Industries trolley buses. In mid-2004 the first 28 low-floor, two-axle Neoplan trolley buses were delivered, one of which is pictured here. The trolley buses use the Harvard Square subway, and like the replaced trolley buses, the new ones have a passenger door on the left side for use in the subway. *Herb Pence*

A trolley bus system was established by the Montreal (Quebec) Tramways in 1937. It was the first in Canada except for experimental services in Windsor and Toronto. Montreal chose the Associated Equipment Co. (AEC) to build its first seven trolley buses, one of which is pictured. They were 40-passenger, six-wheel trolley buses with bodies by Metropolitan-Cammel-Weymann, another British firm. The Montreal system purchased 40 CCF-Brill vehicles in 1947, with more purchases in 1950 and 1952, making a total of 106 new trolley buses.

## Canada

In Canada experimental trolley bus systems began in the early 1920s, in Windsor and Toronto, but they did not last long. Successful trolley bus operations in Canada didn't begin until the late 1930s. A system in Montreal began in 1937 and another in Edmonton in 1939. Both of those systems began with trolley buses imported from England. Winnipeg also started a trolley bus system, in 1938. After World War II more trolley bus systems were established in Canada, making a total of 14 cities operating trolley buses.

The Canadian Car & Foundry Company took on a partnership with the ACF-Brill Company in the United States and built trolley buses in Fort William (now Thunder Bay), Ontario, using the same body styles as American trolley buses. Canadian Car and CCF-Brill built nearly 1,100 trolley buses between 1945 and 1954. An interesting sidelight to the Canadian trolley bus systems was that Nova Scotia Light & Power Company, which began in 1949 in Halifax, had only trolley buses and no street cars or motor buses in its systems through 1969.

In general, trolley bus systems in Canadian cities began somewhat later than those in the United States, but when Canadian systems have closed, they usually lasted longer than their United States equivalents. In 1970, 10 Canadian cities still had trolley bus systems. Four of these continued for a number of years. The systems in Toronto and Hamilton both closed in the early 1990s. The two systems closed even after replacing their old vehicles with new trolley buses built by Flyer Industries in Winnipeg.

The only trolley bus systems in Canada today are in Edmonton and Vancouver. Edmonton acquired new trolley buses built using a unique arrangement where Brown Boveri furnished the electrical equipment and General Motors of Canada built the bodies. Vancouver acquired a number of new trolley buses from Flyer Industries in the 1980s and now has a contract with New Flyer Industries for 147 standard and 40 articulated trolley buses. Some Canadian cities have talked about returning to trolley buses but nothing has developed.

The Winnipeg (Manitoba) Electric Company was the second transit system in Canada to begin operating a modern trolley bus system. Winnipeg had the first fleet of North American-built trolley buses in Canada. (The first modern system, in Montreal, operated seven AEC trolley buses from England. There had been two short-lived trolley bus operations in Canada in the early 1920s.) In 1938, 11 Model CR Mack trolley buses were purchased. The first one is pictured here. In 1940 and 1943, ten more Mack trolley buses were purchased. Later Pullman-Standard and CCF-Brill trolley buses were added. Trolley bus service in Winnipeg continued until 1970. *Lewis B. Foote photograph from the City of Winnipeg Transit System Archive Collection*

The Nova Scotia Light and Power Company in Halifax discontinued street car service in 1949. Late in 1948, five CCF-Brill Model T-44 trolley buses were purchased for the changeover. In the next six years 20 more CCF-Brill trolley buses were added to the fleet. In 1955, the Angus L. MacDonald suspension bridge was completed, linking Halifax with the community of Dartmouth across Halifax Harbor. At the time it was the second-longest suspension bridge in the British Empire. Trolley bus service across the bridge began when it opened. This picture shows three 1952 CCF-Brill trolley buses parked on the bridge three months before the opening to publicize the forthcoming trolley bus service. Trolley bus service in Halifax ended in 1969. *Paul Leger*

On a cold winter day this CCF-Brill Model T-44 trolley bus is pictured operating on the St. Mary's route in Winnipeg, Manitoba. It was one of 39 trolley buses delivered in 1948. Twenty-five similar vehicles entered service the previous year. Others were added later, making a total of 104 CCF-Brill trolley buses in the Winnipeg fleet. Winnipeg was one of the few cities in Canada that had new trolley buses from four different manufacturers. When this picture was taken, the Winnipeg system came under municipal ownership and was known as the Metropolitan Corporation of Greater Winnipeg. Trolley bus service in Winnipeg ended in 1970.

Port Arthur (Ontario) Utilities replaced its aging street car fleet with 10 CCF-Brill Model C-44 trolley buses in 1947. One is pictured here. Port Arthur was adjacent to Fort William, the city where CCF-Brill built 1,098 trolley buses between 1945 and 1954. A joint trolley bus service, the Main Line, connected the two cities. Trolley buses operated in Port Arthur and Fort William until 1972 when the two cities merged to become the city of Thunder Bay.

Although Toronto, Ontario, had four trolley buses in service from 1922 to 1925, the city's modern trolley bus system began in 1947, when the Toronto Transit Commission (TTC) acquired 75 CCF-Brill Model T-44 trolley buses. Ten similar vehicles were added the next year, and 40 Model CCF-Brill T-48A vehicles in 1953. Toronto also added used Marmon-Herrington trolley buses from Cincinnati in 1953 and from Cleveland in 1963. When trolley bus replacement became necessary in the 1970s, TTC ordered 151 trolley buses from Flyer Industries (New Flyer Industries) of Winnipeg, Manitoba, with some of the motors and electrical equipment coming from Toronto's CCF-Brill trolley buses. One of the 1971 Flyer trolley buses is pictured. Trolley bus operations in Toronto ended in 1993.

Trolley bus service in Hamilton, Ontario, began in 1950 by the Hamilton Street Railway Company. Original trolley buses were 18 Model T-48 CCF-Brill vehicles. Thirty CCF-Brill T-48A trolley buses were added in 1951. In 1972, when it became necessary to renew the fleet, Hamilton ordered 40 Flyer Industries trolley buses. Motors and controls for the new vehicles were from the retired CCF-Brill trolley buses in the fleet plus some from Thunder Bay, which closed its trolley bus system the same year. One of the new trolley buses that went into service in 1978 is pictured. Trolley bus service in Hamilton continued until 1992.

Pictured is the prototype of 188, 40-foot New Flyer Model E40LF trolley buses in the process of being delivered to the Coast Mountain Bus Company, operator of buses and trolley buses in the Vancouver, British Columbia, area. The Coast Mountain Bus Company is a subsidiary of the Greater Vancouver Transportation Authority. In addition to the 40-foot trolley buses, forty 60-foot articulated trolley buses are included in the order. These new trolley buses will have batteries that will allow the vehicles to operate off-wire when necessary. The Model E40LF trolley buses will replace 232 Flyer Model E0-2 trolley buses. The trolley bus system in Vancouver began in 1948. It is one of two systems in Canada that have continued.

Edmonton (Alberta) Transit began its trolley bus system in 1939. The service began with six trolley buses from England, three AEC trolley buses with Metropolitan-Cammel-Weymann bodies, and three Leyland trolley buses with Park Royal bodies. Over the years a number of manufacturers sold trolley buses to Edmonton and some used trolley buses were acquired. In 1981-1982, 100 new trolley buses were purchased from Brown Boveri of Canada. The electrical and operating equipment was by Brown Boveri and the bodies were from the Diesel Division of General Motors of Canada. One of these trolley buses is pictured. Although there have been reports that trolley bus service would end at any time in Edmonton, the service has continued, but with a smaller fleet than the 137 vehicles at its peak.

Vancouver, British Columbia, has had the largest trolley bus system in Canada, and continues to operate trolley buses with a sizable fleet. In 1982-1983, the fleet was updated with 245 Flyer Industries Model E901A and E902 trolley buses. One of these trolley buses is pictured operating on Granville Street in downtown Vancouver. At the time, the Metro Transit Operating Company in Vancouver operated the trolley buses. These trolley buses are being replaced with new trolley buses produced by New Flyer Industries, which is the updated name for Flyer Industries.

The city of Mexico City had the first and only trolley bus system in Mexico until 1977. It began in 1951 and continues today. Outside of 20 new trolley buses built by Westram in the United States, most Mexico City trolley buses were used vehicles from cities in the United States that had discontinued trolley bus services. In 1979 Mexico City received its first trolley buses built in Mexico. They were built by Mexicana de Autobuses, SA (MASA) in Tultitlan. Since that time new Mexico City trolley buses have been built by MASA, the only Mexican firm that has built trolley buses. Pictured is a 1984 MASA Model 5501T operating in Mexico City.

## Mexico

Mexico City began a trolley bus trial in 1951 with a small number of used vehicles from the United States. The system in Mexico City still continues to operate. The use of secondhand vehicles has allowed the capital to construct and operate a huge system at an affordable cost. Some of its vehicles have lasted, with rebuilding, for more than 30 years. In recent years, most of the trolley buses used in Mexico City have been built by the Mexican firm Mexicana de Autobuses, SA de CV (MASA), which has built more than 800 trolley buses.

Pollution is a major concern in the Mexican capital. Its system features trunk trolley bus routes in exclusive lanes. Political developments resulted in growth and expansion during the 1980s. Since then there has been some downsizing.

The only other system in Mexico is in Guadalajara. Operations began there with a secondhand fleet from Chicago running two routes through a tunnel designed for light-rail vehicles. The light-rail system was completed, and the outer position of the tunnel routes have been connected to each other and serve, in part, as a feeder system to the light rail. Other cross-town services also are operated. The system in Guadalajara operated 100 trolley buses built by MASA.

The Sistema de Transporte Colectivo de la Zona Metropolitana (Sistecozome) operates the trolley bus system in Guadalajara, Mexico. Trolley buses were introduced in 1977 with used vehicles from the United States. Pictured is one of the Marmon-Herrington trolley buses in service in Guadalajara. These trolley buses were built in 1951/52 and operated in the Chicago (Illinois) Transit fleet for a number of years. Guadalajara's trolley bus fleet now numbers more than 100 trolley buses, all built by the Mexican firm MASA. *Wilhelm Pflug*

Pictured is one of the 170 MASA Model STE trolley buses acquired by the Servicdo de Transportes Electricos del Distrito Federal in Mexico City from 1979 to 1981. The trolley bus system in Mexico City is the largest system in North America. It began in 1951 and continues. There are 17 routes that in 1999 carried 64.5 million passengers. Extensions of the Metro in Mexico City replaced trolley bus routes in some areas while other routes have been extended or started anew. *Loring M. Lawrence*

Guadalajara, Mexico, began operating trolley buses in 1977, and the service continues. Pictured is one of the 100 Model 5500T trolley buses built by Mexicana de Autobuses SA (MASA) between 1984 and 1988. Sistema de Transporte Colectivo de la Zona Metropolitana operates the system. *Wilhelm Pflug*

# South America

## *Argentina*

There are currently three systems in operation in Argentina. In the mid-1950s there were trolley bus systems in several Argentinean cities. The one in Buenos Aires was very large and purchased a large number of trolley buses.

The city of Rosario managed to keep its trolley buses operating by putting its old but reliable electrical equipment into new vehicles. The city received a new fleet and a new operator in 1994. The city of Mendoza began service in 1958 with Soviet-made ZIU trolley buses. In recent years Mendoza has also acquired used trolley buses from Solingen, Germany. The most recent new system to open was in the city of Cordoba, which began operation in 1989, using a combination of new vehicles and a fleet of used Soviet vehicles and German vehicles from Solingen.

All trolley buses in Argentina have been imported, mainly from the United States, Italy, Germany, Great Britain, China, and Russia.

Mendoza, Argentina, is one of the three cities in Argentina that continue to operate trolley buses. The system had its start in 1958. In 1962, 36 Japanese-built Nissan trolley buses were purchased, some of which operated into the mid-1990s. In 1984, 17 Soviet-built Uritsky ZIU trolley buses were acquired. One is pictured here in 1986.

The trolley bus system in Mendoza, Argentina, operated by Empresa Provincial de Transporte de Mendoza (EPTM), acquired 78 trolley buses from the Stadtwerke Solingen (Germany) in 1989. Krupp/Ludewig in Germany built these trolley buses between 1968 and 1974 for the Solingen system. Krupp was not the largest builder of trolley buses in Germany and only built 23 trolley buses, other than the 80 that were built for Solingen. The Solingen trolley buses were among the last built by Krupp. Pictured is one of the Krupp/Ludewig trolley buses operating in Mendoza in 1998.

## Brazil

Historically, trolley bus systems did not begin in Brazil until quite late. The first trolley bus system opened there in 1949 and the next ones didn't begin until 10 years later. Early trolley buses were imported, but by the end of the 1950s Brazil had developed its own type of vehicles along North American lines. System expansions occurred in the late 1950s and early 1960s, but some operations did not last long.

The trolley bus system in Sao Paulo experienced the most growth of any system in the country. In fact, Sao Paulo had several companies operating trolley buses and several private companies acquired from the government in 1994 continue to do so. At one time the city had more than 1,000 trolley buses in service. Sao Paulo has advanced several innovative ideas: a trial using three-phase alternating current; segregated trolley bus lanes with offside high platforms; and double-articulated vehicles with doors on both sides for use with high platforms.

In recent years there was a plan to begin an ultra-modern trolley bus busway system in Sao Paulo. The roadway and the trolley bus overhead were completed, but the planned use of trolley buses was discontinued and it is expected motor buses will operate the new busway. The trolley buses designed for this system were biarticulated vehicles of ultramodern design. They were tested extensively in Sao Paulo, although the system never began.

In addition to Sao Paulo, at the present time there are two other systems in Brazil, in the cities of Santos and Recife. The city of Araraquara used trolley buses for all its local transport service until the late 1980s, when a number of routes were converted to motor buses.

Several manufacturers in Brazil, particularly Marcopolo and Busscar, have built trolley buses over the years.

Rio Claro, Brazil, had a trolley bus operation that began in 1986. It lasted only seven years. The trolley bus pictured is a rebuilt 1966 ODC trolley bus from Sao Paulo's CMTC system. Four other used trolley buses were acquired from Sao Paulo. The system was never a success and closed in 1993. *Allen Morrison*

From 1979 to 1981, 200 of these trolley buses went into service in Sao Paulo, Brazil. They were built by Scania and had Ciferal bodies. The Companhia Municipal de Transportes Colectivos (CMTC), a municipal department, operated these trolley buses until the system was privatized in 1994. Electrobus assumed some of the service and these trolley buses, which have now been retired, were included in the changeover in 1994.

This Marcopolo-bodied Scania articulated trolley bus, the only one of its type, was delivered in 1985 to the Companhia Municipal de Transportes Colectivos (CMTC), in Sao Paulo, Brazil, in 1985. At that time the CMTC had a fleet of 500 trolley buses. In 1994 the municipal operation was privatized. The trolley bus system continued, with private companies owning the vehicles and becoming responsible for vehicle operation and maintenance. CMTC was the oldest trolley system in Brazil, beginning in 1949.

Companhia Santida de Transports Colectivos (CSTC) in Santos, Brazil, began operating trolley buses in 1963 and the service continues. In 1981, 10 of these Marcopolo-bodied Scania trolley buses were delivered. At one time the Santos trolley bus system had 50 vehicles and six routes, but in recent years service has been reduced to one route with seven trolley buses. One report indicated that 30 new trolley buses were being considered. The original Santos trolley buses were Italian Alfa Romeo/Fiat vehicles similar to those in service in other South American cities.

Electrobus was the private company in Brazil that assumed a number of the trolley bus routes in Sao Paulo when the municipal CMTC organization elected to privatize the trolley bus service. Electrobus became the operator of 95 of these Marcopolo Torino trolley buses in 1996. They had Scania Latin America chassis. Electrobus also became the owner of 60 similar trolley buses, but with Volvo do Brasil B58 chassis.

Sao Paulo, Brazil, has been a city very favorable to trolley buses for many years. Brazil and other South American countries have felt busways were a way for the future of urban transportation. At ExpoBus in Sao Paulo in 1998, this futuristic biarticulated trolley bus was first shown. A fleet of 31 of these vehicles was scheduled to begin operating in Sao Paulo on a new-guided busway with raised platforms. It was supposed to be operational by 2002, but political and other problems have interfered, and the future of this trolley bus operation is uncertain.

## Chile

The only two trolley bus systems operated in Chile were in the cities of Santiago and Valparaiso. The same company began both. The system in the capital, Santiago, only operated from 1947 to 1948, with 100 Pullman-Standard trolley buses built in the United States and 100 French Vetra vehicles with bodies similar to the Pullman-Standards. In 1990 Chile received a demonstrator trolley bus from China, the first such export from that country. A small order was placed, which, along with some used vehicles, allowed service to begin again in Santiago in 1991, although it ended shortly after. It appears now that trolley buses will not again see service in Santiago because of a new ambitious busway system announced recently.

In Valparaiso the French builder Societe des Vehicules et Tracteurs Electriques (Vetra) supplied the vehicles for the original fleet that began operating in 1952. The system still operates today, and is probably one of the most interesting trolley bus systems in the world. The city acquired a number of used trolley buses from Switzerland. At first all the Swiss trolley buses still had Swiss livery, and seeing the buses of various colors coming down the streets of Valparaiso one could tell exactly which Swiss city each vehicle came from.

Valparaiso operates the oldest continually operating trolley bus ever built, one from the original fleet acquired by Santiago in 1947.

The trolley bus pictured is a Pullman-Standard model built in the United States in 1947. It is the oldest trolley bus in the world that continues to operate. It began service in 1947 in Santiago, Chile, and operated there until 1978. It is currently being operated by the Empresa de Transportes Colectivo Electricos in Valparaiso, Chile. A fire damaged the trolley bus in August 2003, but it was repaired and returned to service four months later. This picture was taken in 1998, a year after this trolley bus celebrated 50 years of service.

The trolley bus system in Valparaiso is the only one presently operating in Chile. It has the distinction of having some of the oldest trolley buses in service in the world. Thirty Pullman-Standard Model 48CX vehicles were delivered from the United States to Valparaiso in 1952. Pictured is one of the original Pullman-Standard trolley buses in 1998.

This Berna trolley bus was put into service in Schaffhausen, Switzerland, in 1965 by the Verkehrsbetriebe der Stadt Schaffhausen. It operated there until it was acquired for service in Valparaiso, Chile, along with several other Swiss trolley buses from Bern and Zurich. The Valparaiso system is operated by the Empresa de Transportes Colectivo Electricos. Other Schaffhausen Berna trolley buses have also been seen in service in Valparaiso.

## Colombia

Trolley bus service in the city of Medellin began in 1929. It was the only city in Colombia with trolley bus service until 1948, when a system began in the capital, Bogota. Service in Medellin was abandoned in 1951. Bogota began service in 1948 with new and used U.S.-made vehicles, but later bought vehicles from Russia and Romania. The Bogota system continued until 1991.

## Ecuador

Trolley bus service in Ecuador began in 1993 with a new system in Quito, the capital. Its system is basically a trolley bus busway system. The vehicles have high floors for loading from high platforms only. The stations are accessible only after paying for a ticket and passing through a barrier. Vehicles are built on Mercedes-Benz chassis with bodies assembled in Spain by Hispano. AEG supplies the electrical equipment. Although all the Quito trolley buses have auxiliary diesel engines, the city, with its high elevation, chose to operate trolley buses to keep vehicle pollution at a minimum. It has been a very successful system. The success of the busway system encouraged the establishment of other reserved busway services in Quito, but improvements to diesel engines kept further trolley bus extensions from being made.

In the 1990s, Quito, Ecuador, was faced with serious environmental and congestion concerns. City officials decided to build a busway on a main corridor through the city. Trolley buses were chosen for the busway service because of the abundance of electric power and the need at that time to control emissions in the city, which has an altitude of 9,000 feet (2,764 meters). Initially, 54 Mercedes-Benz trolley buses with Spanish Hispano Carrocera bodies and Kiepe electric components were the choice. Pictured is one of the original trolley buses at one of the newly built terminals.

A second order for trolley buses for Quito, Ecuador, was made in 2000, and 59 more Mercedes-Benz/Hispano Carrocera trolley buses were delivered. The success of the original trolley bus busway and extensions prompted the need for additional vehicles. One of the second groups of Quito trolley buses is seen on the reserved street in the Old Town.

Trolley buses in Quito, Ecuador, have high platform doors. Each of the 39 stations has high platforms for passenger access to the trolley buses. One of the second groups of Mercedes-Benz/Hispano Carrocera trolley buses is pictured approaching the Calzado Station. All the trolley buses in Quito have auxiliary diesel engines; those in the first order had 175-horsepower engines and the second order had 240-horsepower engines. Further busways have been opened in Quito but they are operated with diesel buses because of improvements in diesel engine emissions.

## Peru

In Lima, Peru, trolley buses entered service as early as 1928. However, the system only operated for a short time and was very small. After its closure, at least one and possibly all six of the vehicles were then mounted on two-axle tramcar trucks that operated until the 1950s.

## Trinidad

One of the most obscure trolley bus systems of the British Empire was in Port of Spain, capital of the West Indian island of Trinidad. It was the only trolley bus system in the Caribbean. It began in 1941 and ended in 1956.

## Uruguay

Uruguay is a small country, but the trolley bus system that began in its capital, Montevideo, in 1951, was relatively large. It used mostly British and Italian-made vehicles, including 40 articulated models. These were the only articulated trolley buses on the South American continent until a few deliveries to Bogota, Sao Paulo, and Cordoba. The system closed early in 1992 when financing deteriorated.

## Venezuela

A system is planned for Merida, a town that is quite hilly and well suited for trolley buses. Hispano Carrocera SA in Zaragoza, Spain, has built 45 trolley buses for the system when it begins service. This will be the newest system in South America. Caracas had a relatively small trolley bus system that lasted only about 10 years beginning in 1937. It has been recently announced that a new trolley bus system will open in mid 2007 in Barquisimento, Venezuela's fourth largest city.

The Administracion Municipal de Transportes Colectivos de Montevideo, in Montevideo, Uruguay, began a trolley bus system in 1951. Original trolley buses were 18 British United Traction (BUT) units, one of which is pictured. These vehicles had bodies by Park Royal Vehicles, another British firm. Trolley bus service in Montevideo lasted for 51 years, and at one time more than 300 trolley buses were operated in the Uruguay capital city.

A cooperative transportation organization named Coop-trol began operating the remainder of the large trolley bus system in Montevideo, Uruguay, in 1986. At the time the trolley bus fleet consisted of 50 Alfa Romeo standard and 18 articulated vehicles, which was considerably fewer vehicles than in previous years. One of the two-axle Alfa Romeo trolley buses is pictured operating in downtown Montevideo in 1986. These vehicles first went into service in the late 1950s.

Merida, Venezuela, decided a few years ago to operate a trolley bus system. Although 45 articulated trolley buses built by Hispano Carrocera in Zaragoza, Spain, have been delivered to the city, the start of the system has been delayed. The initial route is 18.2 kilometers on a long grade. Other routes may be operated. Merida is 800 to 1,800 meters (2,650 to 5,900 feet) in elevation and this will be a most interesting system when it gets underway. Pictured is one of the 45 new trolley buses. The name the system will be using is "Triolmerida." *Gustavo A. Marqueta-Siibert Larrayad, Hispano Carrocera, SA*

# Europe

Europe had the most significant trolley bus systems anywhere in the world. Early trolley buses in Europe began with many experiments, some as early as the 19th Century, particularly in Germany, France, and Italy. Over the years, 75 different cities in Germany have had trolley buses, but only three systems remain. Fifty cities had trolley bus systems in the United Kingdom, 54 in Italy, and 33 in France.

There also have been many trolley bus manufacturers in Europe. These manufacturers provided trolley buses for their own countries as well as exporting trolley buses to other European countries and many other areas of the world. Great Britain was one of the largest builders of trolley buses, although German manufacturers were also quite active in trolley bus manufacturing. In modern times trolley bus manufacturing has been very active in Russia, Ukraine, Czech Republic, and Poland.

The biggest expansion of trolley bus service in Europe has been in Russia, where many cities, both large and small, have trolley bus systems. Service continues in most cities of Russia; very few systems have been discontinued. Other countries of the former Soviet Union have also been important in trolley bus operations, including Ukraine, Belarus, and others. Eastern European trolley bus service has been strong in the Czech Republic, Slovakia, the Baltics, and the Balkans. Some new systems have been established in other European countries, particularly Sweden and Italy. Europe also continues to be very prominent in new technologies in trolley bus operation, manufacturing, and development.

## Western Europe
### Austria

In Austria pioneers developed their own patented current collection system that was used within the Austrian Empire as well as in northern Europe and northern Africa. Although there were trolley bus systems in all the large cities in Austria, only Linz, Salzburg, and Innsbruck continue to operate trolley buses, although the Innsbruck system is expected to be discontinued very soon to be replaced by light rail.

The system begun in 1940 in Salzburg has grown to be the largest trolley bus system in Austria and one of the most progressive in Europe. The other system, in Linz, has operated since 1944.

The Austrian manufacturer Graf & Stift has traditionally built most of Austria's trolley buses and has also exported many to other countries. Some trolley buses have been imported into Austria especially in recent years now that the European Union competitive rules exist. Graf & Stift has been taken over by Mercedes-Benz and the Austrian facility continues trolley bus building.

The Grazer Stadtwerke AG in Graz, Austria, began operating trolley bus service in 1941. The first trolley buses, which were built in 1940, were MAN Model VDK-01 vehicles. One of the six that was delivered in 1941 is pictured here. Graz had a small fleet of trolley buses that only operated two routes. *Peter Schmied*

The Innsbrucker Verkehrsbetriebe AG in Innsbruck, Austria, began a trolley bus service in 1944. The first trolley buses in Innsbruck were from the STU operation in Livorno, Italy. This trolley bus, pictured in Innsbruck, was built by Fiat. It operated until 1972. This Innsbruck system closed in 1976, but the trolley bus service was reinstated in 1988 and continues.

The Murztaler Verkehrs Gesellschaft (MVG) of Kapfenberg, Austria, had a small intercity trolley bus line beginning in 1944. Most of the trolley buses that operated the system were acquired from other systems. This articulated MVG trolley bus, a Henschel 175 160 OSL, was built in 1961. Before it came to the MVG in 1974 it served in Aachen and Bielefeld, Germany. The MVG trolley bus service ended in 2002.

Twin cities of Bruck an der Mur and Kapfenberg in Styria, Austria, operated trolley buses from 1944 through 2002. Murztaler Verkehrs Gesellschaft (MVG) operated the system. This Graf & Stift Model OE 100/54 trolley bus of 1957 is one of the few vehicles acquired new for the system.
*Wilhelm Pflug*

In 1948 the Grazer Stadtwerke of Graz, Austria, added five Model EO Graf & Stift trolley buses to the six MAN trolley buses that began the service in 1941. One of these Graf & Stift trolley buses is pictured. They operated in Graz until the service was discontinued in 1967. *Peter Schmied*

Stadtwerke Klagenfurt-Verkehrsbetriebe (KVB) in Klagenfurt, Austria, began a trolley bus system in 1944 with eight trolley buses. One of the eight Henschel Model C trolley buses that was operated by the system is pictured. The Klagenfurt trolley bus system ended in 1963. *Harald Herrmann*

The trolley bus system in Salzburg, Austria, has been, and still is, the largest system in Austria. It was started by the Salzburger Stadtwerke Verkehrsbetriebe with 10 MAN Model MPE1 trolley buses. The German firm MAN built the first 20 Salzburg trolley buses. Two later MAN trolley buses, each pulling trailers, are pictured at the Staatsbrucke with the famous Salzburg Castle on the hill in the background.

Vienna, Austria's Wiener Stadtwerke-Verkehrsbetriebe had two trolley bus systems, each of which had only one route. One system operated from 1908 to 1938. The second began in 1946. It was small in comparison with other large-city trolley bus systems, and ended in 1968. This system had 10 trolley buses built by Henschel & Sohn GmbH of Kassel, Germany. One of them is pictured on Route 22, which was an outlying rural route.

The Innsbrucker Verkehrsbetriebe AG in Innsbruck, Austria, began a trolley bus service in 1944. It closed in 1976, but was restarted in 1988 over a different route, and continues today. When the new system began in 1988, 16 Austrian Graf & Stift/Kiepe Model GE 150 M 18 articulated trolley buses went into service. One of these is pictured here.

Linzer Elektrizitats-Fernwarme und Verkehrsbetriebe, Linz, Austria, is one of three trolley bus systems continuing to operate in Austria. At one time there were eight trolley bus systems in that country. Pictured is a 1960 Graf & Stift Model GEO 1 articulated trolley bus, one of 20 of this type that operated in Linz. The Graf & Stift trolley buses of 1960 had a distinctive frontal appearance.

The Steyr-Daimler-Puch AG vehicle manufacturing company in Austria had its beginnings back in 1922, but operated under different names until 1935. The company built buses, but only 12 trolley buses. Four of the Steyr trolley buses, one of which is pictured here, had Kiepe electrics and were sold to Linzer Elektrizitats-Fernwarme und Verkehrsbetriebe in Linz, Austria, in 1988. The trolley bus service in Linz began in 1944 and continues. Graf & Stift, the important builder of Austrian trolley buses, had built most of the Linz trolley buses. Today, Linz runs a fleet of Volvo trolley buses built in Poland.

This Austrian-built Graf & Stift 3-axle articulated trolley bus, Model NGT204M165, was one of six delivered to Salzburger Stadtwerke Aktiengesellschaft Verkehrsbetriebe, Salzburg, Austria, in 1997. In the two previous years 14 similar trolley buses had been added. Except for one other trolley bus of this type, which went to Kapfenberg, Austria, all were in the Salzburg fleet. Articulated trolley buses were first used in Salzburg in 1961. Graf & Stift built some and others were German Henschel trolley buses. This trolley bus is making the turn to cross the Staatsbrucke in the center of Salzburg.

It wasn't until the 1970s that Steyr-Daimler-Puch AG of Vienna placed importance on building buses. One of the 12 trolley buses the company built is pictured here. It and three others went into service in Salzburg, Austria, for the Salzburger Stadtwerke in 1988. The Austrian manufacturer Graf & Stift built other trolley buses in the Salzburg fleet at the time.

Salzburg, Austria, with its Stadt bus, has been one of the world's most progressive trolley bus systems. It recently celebrated 65 years of trolley buses. Since the system first began in 1940 there has been regular modernization. In 2000 a Van Hool Model AG300T trolley bus was acquired, and in 2002, 2003, and 2005, 19 more of the same model were added. One of the 2003 Van Hool trolley buses is pictured emerging from the Sigmundstor near the city center.

## Belgium

Belgium has had five trolley bus systems, two of which started very early, in 1929 and 1930. Brussels and Antwerp had small trolley bus systems, and Liege had a large system. The last trolley buses ceased operations in Belgium in 1971, but the interest in their export potential and environmental trends convinced the government to make funds available for a new installation in Ghent. The system opened in 1989 with Belgian-built Van Hool articulated trolley buses.

In the southwestern Liege suburbs a separate company, Les Railways Economiques de Liege-Seraing et Extensions, SA (RELSE), ran a small system employing unique reversible trolley buses, with controls at both ends. The vehicles were later rebuilt to conventional single-ended layout. Another interesting vehicle that operated in the Liege area was a three-axle trolley bus, with one of the three axles in the very middle of the vehicle. One of these is preserved in a Belgium museum.

Vehicles from Britain initially influenced Belgium trolley bus services, but the country built up an important trolley bus manufacturing business itself. Prominent early manufacturers were Brossel and Fabrique Nationale D'Armes de Guerre, SA (FN), both of which no longer produce trolley buses. The Van Hool company, a leading builder of motor buses in Belgium, also builds trolley buses and has supplied a number of them to various countries. One significant Van Hool order came from Athens, Greece, for new trolley buses to help modernize its system for the Summer Olympics in 2004.

The Belgian firm Brossel built this 1938 double-ended trolley bus. It was one of two that were put into service by Les Railways Economiques de Liege-Seraing et Extensions, SA (RELSE) in Seraing, Belgium. These two trolley buses were probably the smallest ever built, seating about 20 persons. It was double ended; that is, it could be driven from both ends and the trolley poles could be rotated. The RELSE system began in 1936 and closed in 1963. It was a small system with a maximum of 10 trolley buses.

Tramwegen van Antwerpen en Omgeving, Antwerp, Belgium, began the first trolley bus service in Belgium in 1929. A Minerva trolley bus was one of the first to operate in Antwerp. In 1938, 15 trolley buses, one of which is pictured here, went into service in Antwerp. They were built by Fabrique Nationale d'Armes de Guerre SA (FN). The Antwerp system was not a large one and closed in 1964.

The trolley bus service of Les Railways Economiques de Liege-Seraing et Extensions, SA (RELSE) in Seraing, Belgium, had some of the smallest and most unusual trolley buses ever built. Four of these vehicles were delivered in 1936. They had three axles, one of which was situated in the middle of the vehicle. The poles could be swung around and the trolley bus could be operated in either direction without turning around. They were built in Belgium by Brossel. One of these trolley buses has been preserved and is in a transportation museum in Belgium.

Seraing, a suburban city of Liege, Belgium, had a small trolley bus system operated by the Societe des Transports Intercommunaux de Liege-Seraing. The service began within the Seraing area in 1936 and was discontinued in 1968. Pictured is one of the several Brossel trolley buses that were operated by the Liege Seraing undertaking in 1946.

In 1954 the Societe des Transports Intercommunaux de l'Agglomeration Liegeoise, Liege, Belgium, had 30 of these trolley buses built by Fabrique Nationale d'Armes de Guerre SA (FN). Liege was one of four Belgian cities that operated trolley buses. The Liege system was the first in Belgium, beginning in 1930. It was a large system, with 140 trolley buses in service in 1963. Trolley buses were discontinued in Liege in 1971.

Ghent has the only trolley bus system presently operating in Belgium. It began in 1989 with 20 Van Hool Model AG 300 T articulated trolley buses. Pictured is one of these vehicles traveling on one of downtown Ghent's cobblestone streets. The trolley bus route passes many of the historic buildings in Ghent. Recently, the trolley bus service in Ghent was suspended while new one-way street construction was underway, but service has been reinstated.

## France

France and Germany were similar in their development of the trolley bus in its early days. There were five or six experimental trolley bus systems in France in the early part of the 20th Century. Most of these did not survive long. It wasn't until the very late 1920s and 1930s that trolley bus systems began regular services. There were a few large systems, such as Lyon and Marseille, but most of the systems begun after World War II were modest, short-lived operations.

The system in Lyon, which began in 1935, was one of largest early systems and remains one of the largest systems in France today. It now operates new Cristalis trolley buses built by Irisbus, among the most modern trolley buses currently being manufactured. St. Etienne is also modernizing its trolley bus system with new Cristalis trolley buses. Three other trolley bus systems continue to operate in France, although the one in Marseille appears to have a limited future.

Paris had some trolley bus services between 1943 and 1966, despite the fact that overhead wires were banned in certain areas of the capital. Only four routes in the outlying areas of Paris were operated by trolley buses.

An interesting version of trolley bus service was established in recent years in Nancy, which at one time had conventional trolley buses. This vehicle is a rubber-tired tram that operates with overhead power and has a conduit in the street for guidance. The city of Caen also has a rubber-tired electrical-type trolley bus, but it has only one overhead power line and has a return in a conduit. These trolley buses have auxiliary diesel engines that power them over a portion of the routes. They have an auxiliary power source, which allows them to operate off the conduit and into the workshop. The rubber tires help them to negotiate hills with ease.

Most of the early trolley bus vehicles in France were supplied by Vetra, an important early French trolley bus manufacturer, and the largest producer of trolley buses in France. There were also a number of other significant trolley bus manufacturers there. Trolley buses were exported to other countries in Europe and cities in North Africa and elsewhere.

Irisbus, which was formed a few years ago by several European manufacturers, including the French company Renault, builds ultramodern Cristalis trolley buses that are now in service in Lyon and St. Etienne. The large electrical company Alstom (formerly Alstrom) has been providing the motors and electrical equipment for many trolley buses in the past as well as now.

Mulhouse, France, had two trolley bus systems in the past. One began in 1908 and operated with four vehicles for 10 years. The second system was started in 1947 by the Transports en Commun de Mulhouse. It operated 21 trolley buses until 1969. One of the eight original vehicles was this Model VBR trolley bus built by Vetra in 1947. Eleven Somua trolley buses were added in 1950, and two more Vetras came in 1952. *Malcolm Chase*

Pictured is a Vetra Model VBH85, one of 21 that were delivered to the Compagnie des Omnibus et Tramways de Lyon SA in Lyon, France, in 1963. Societe des Vehicules et Travaux Electriques (Vetra) was organized in 1925 and manufactured more than 1,700 trolley buses. Most of these went to French systems, but many were exported. Renault supplied chassis for early Vetra trolley buses and later, when integral construction began, supplied only the running gear. When this Vetra Model VBH was built the bodies were a product of Automobiles M. Berliet, an important French builder of automobiles and trucks. Lyon began operating trolley buses in 1935 and service continues today with a fleet of 87 modern vehicles. *Nicolas Tellier*

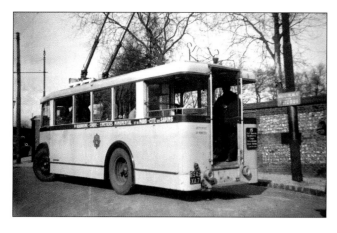

Trolley buses served in Rouen, France, from 1933 until 1970. The city is quite hilly; therefore, trolley buses were very suitable. Compagnie des Tramways de Rouen operated Route 15 where this Vetra Model CS35 trolley bus began service in 1936. Five similar trolley buses were acquired between 1934 and 1937 for three different routes. They had an unusual rear entrance and an open standing area at the rear. Later these trolley buses were rebuilt when one-man operations began. *Werner Kutil*

Place Dorian, in the center of Saint-Etienne, France, has been an important meeting place for the trolley buses of Tramways Elec-triques de Saint-Etienne (TE) for many years. The trolley bus in the foreground is one of 56 Vetra Model VCR vehicles that were in the Saint-Etienne fleet. The other two trolley buses were Model ELR Berliets. Saint-Etienne had 40 of these trolley buses. Service with trolley buses began in Saint-Etienne in 1942 and continues today. This picture was taken 30 years ago.

The Companie des Tramways de Rouen (CTR), France, operated a trolley bus system beginning in 1933 and continuing for 37 years. The original trolley buses were Vetra Model CS 60 vehicles. Eleven of the original trolley buses in the fleet were modernized in the Rouen shops in 1957-1958. Two of the refurbished trolley buses that resulted are pictured in downtown Rouen. Rouen has some hill routes, therefore, trolley buses performed very well. *Werner Kutil, Connex*

In 1957 the Regie Autonome des Transports Parisiens (RATP) of Paris, France, bought 38 Vetra Model VBF trolley buses, one of which is pictured here. Paris had three different trolley bus experiences. The first operated from 1912 to 1914 with two trolley buses. The second began in 1925 and lasted for 10 years. A larger trolley bus system for Paris began in 1943 and ended in 1966. All trolley buses in the last Paris system were products of Vetra, beginning with the CS60 model. Trolley buses operated by the RATP involved only four routes in the southern and western suburban areas. *Nicolas Tellier*

Pictured traveling along one of the narrow streets in St. Etienne, France, is a Berliet Model E100H trolley bus, one of 25 that were acquired in 1981. Trolley bus service began in St. Etienne in 1942 and continues today. There are seven trolley bus routes, with 50 trolley buses. Automobiles M. Berliet was founded in 1902 and built a variety of automobiles, buses, and trucks. The first trolley buses were built in 1955.

In 1982 trolley buses began operating in Nancy, France. The first trolley buses were 48 dual-mode Renault Model PER180H articulated units. This was one of the first dual-mode systems in the world. The trolley buses operated under wire in the central part of Nancy, and then traveled in the outlying suburban areas under diesel power. Compagnie Generale Francaise des Transport et d'Enterprises operated these trolley buses. This trolley bus service ended in 2001, while a system using Bombardier TVR vehicles was being established.

The Societe des Transports Urbains de l'Agglomeration Stephanoise of St. Etienne, France, has operated trolley buses since 1942, and continues. Pictured is one of the eight Renault Model PER 180H trolley buses that went into service in St. Etienne in 1984. This trolley bus is pictured in 1992 at the Place Dorain bus and trolley bus center in St. Etienne.

The Societe Grenobloise de Tramway Electriques, now the Transports de l'Agglomeration de Grenoble (TAG), France, began trolley bus service in 1947. The first Grenoble trolley buses were Model VBBs built by Vetra. More Vetras were added later. In 1977-1979, 50 Berliet ER100R two-axle trolley buses, one of which is pictured here, joined the Grenoble fleet. Trolley bus service in Grenoble ended in 1999, although there has been some talk of resuming trolley bus service.

Limoges, a city in central France, has had a trolley bus system since 1943. In 1983, 25 new Renault Model ER 100H trolley buses were acquired. One of these trolley buses is pictured in downtown Limoges in 1999. Previously, Vetra trolley buses, originally from Paris, were in service, some of which operated for nearly 40 years. The present Limoges trolley bus system is operated by Transports en Commun de Limoges.

Transports en Commun Lyonnaise (formerly Compagnie des Omnibus et Tramways de Lyon) in Lyon, France, has had trolley bus service since 1935. It has always been the largest trolley bus system in France. When Irisbus announced it was building the ultramodern Cristalis ETB12 trolley bus, Lyon was the first city to place an order. During 2002, 55 of the new 12-meter Cristalis Model ETB1 trolley buses were delivered. Twelve articulated 18-meter Cristalis Model ETB trolley buses were also added to the Lyon fleet. It is interesting to note that the Cristalis models do not have trolley retrievers at the rear. Rewiring, if a pole becomes detached from the overhead wire, requires a long pole to reposition the trolley pole.

Marseilles, France, had one of the earliest trolley bus systems in France. It lasted two years, from 1903 to 1905. In 1942 trolley buses were again introduced to Marseilles, and it became the second-largest system in France, with 162 single-deck trolley buses. The French firm Vetra built some of the first Marseilles trolley buses. Pictured is a Renault Model ER 100 R, one of the 48 delivered in 1979-1980 to the Regie Autonome des Transports de la ville de Marseille. The trolley bus system is in the process of closing at the present time.

This vehicle has characteristics of a trolley bus, a tram, and a bus. It operates by electric power and has rubber tires; therefore, it is very similar to a trolley bus. However, it only operates on electrical power when it follows a single track in the roadway, and has only one overhead wire. An auxiliary diesel engine enables it to travel off the electrical system in certain situations and also to reach the workshop. There are 24 of these units operating in the French city of Caen. They were first introduced in 2002. Compagnie des Transports l'Agglomeration Caennaise (Twisto) operates the system.

Nancy, France, opened a trolley bus system in 1982 with dual-mode vehicles. In 2001 this service was stopped. A new type trolley bus service began afterward, following a series of suspensions due to malfunctions. However, in early 2002, problems were resolved and 25 Bombardier biarticulated vehicles were in service. These trolley buses have low floors throughout, auxiliary diesel engines, and a modern tram-like appearance. They run on rubber tires and operate with a guided single track on some sections, and without the guided track on other sections. Pictured is one of the vehicles in downtown Nancy.

## Germany

The first electric rail-less vehicle, the "elektromote," was produced in Germany in 1882. Nearly 20 years later, patents were obtained in Germany for a reliable current collection system. The early technology was used in small towns and rural systems for freight operations. The success of those systems encouraged others to devise alternative technical solutions.

The typical German trolley bus system was small, and the presence of a larger tram system often meant that when trolley bus renewal became necessary the system was abandoned in the interest of standardization on trams, although some services were replaced with diesel buses.

In the early 1940s trolley buses were used to replace motor buses when fuel and vehicles were scarce. More trolley bus systems opened in the late 1940s, but growth slowed as fuel and new motor buses became more available.

From the late 1950s until 1970 East Germany relied on Skoda trolley buses imported from the Czech Republic. Most of the systems were quite small, with very few having more than 30 or 40 trolley buses. The country went for 13 years without acquiring any new trolley buses, and this nearly caused the total closure of all systems in East Germany. New vehicles from the Czech Republic and Hungary were received in the mid-1980s.

Germany has had a number of important manufacturers of trolley buses, not only for domestic trolley bus systems, but also for export. Important names in German trolley bus manufacturing have been Henschel, Bussing, MAN, Mercedes-Benz, and Neoplan. The latter three continue to build trolley buses.

A number of the suppliers of motors and electrical components for trolley buses have been from Germany, including Kiepe, AEG, and Siemens. One, Kiepe Elektrik GmbH (now Vossloh Kiepe GmbH) has just celebrated 100 years in business. Theodor Kiepe began the business for the repair of electrical arc lamps in 1906. Not only did the company supply electrical equipment for domestic trolley buses, it also exported its products to many countries. In 1952 the company supplied its products for an order of 700 trolley buses for Buenos Aires, Argentina. Most recently, the 142 new trolley buses for Athens, Greece, and the 228 trolley buses going into service in Vancouver, British Columbia, are equipped with electrics from Vossloh Kiepe GmbH.

Trier, Germany, in the Moselle Valley, began trolley bus service in 1939. The maximum extent of the network was reached in 1956 with four routes and 14 kilometers. The fleet reached a total of 31 trolley buses in 1963. The Stadtwerke Trier Abteilung Verkehrsbetriebe trolley bus pictured was one of the original five types MPE built by MAN in 1939. In 1959 this vehicle passed its one million kilometer mark. It was scrapped in 1967 when the closure of the system began. Actual closing of the Trier system came in 1970. *D. A. Jones London Trolley Bus Preservation Society*

Three trolley bus systems operate in Germany today, in Solingen, Eberswalde, and Esslingen. The city of Solingen has always had the largest trolley bus system in Germany. Solingen replaced its trams with trolley buses between 1952 and 1959. A new generation of trolley buses and a major expansion began operating in 1993.

The city of Darmstadt, Germany, which is south of Frankfurt, had two trolley bus routes. The Hessische Elektrizitats AG (HEAG) operated the service. The two routes were not physically connected. The first route, to Ober-Ramstadt, opened in 1944, replacing a nine-kilometer motor bus service. The second route of five kilometers opened a year later. Pictured in 1959 is one of four Henschel/Drauz trolley buses of 1947/48 with a DUWAG trailer at the Bollenfall loop in 1954. HEAG trolley bus service ended in 1963. *D. A. Jones London Trolley Bus Preservation Society*

Nurnberg, Germany's Verkehrs-Aktiengesellschaft (VAG) operated a very small trolley bus service that only required eight vehicles. The service began in 1948 with a six-kilometer route that replaced motor buses. Another route followed in 1949. Pictured is one of the eight MAN Model MKE trolley buses used in Nurnberg. Trailers were used in peak periods. VAG began operating the Nurnberg-Further Strassenbahn service in 1959. The trolley bus service in Nurnberg ceased in 1962. *D. A. Jones London Trolley Bus Preservation Society*

Trolley bus service of the Dortmunder Stadtwerke AG in Dortmund, Germany, had its beginning in 1962 on a seven-kilometer route. It replaced a motor bus service. The system reached its peak in 1960 when there were three routes with a combined length of 81 kilometers. The closing of the trolley bus system started in 1962, and the last trolley bus ran in 1967. Pictured is one of eight small 1948 Henschel/Kassbohrer/SSW trolley buses that operated in Dortmund. Articulated trolley buses were first operated in Dortmund in 1958. *D. A. Jones London Trolley Bus Preservation Society*

Stadtwerke Hildesheim AG in Hildesheim, Germany, began a trolley bus system in 1943 that continued to operate in Hildesheim until 1969. The German firm Henschel & Sohn AG, an important truck and bus builder in Kassel, built all the new trolley buses that were in service. The trolley bus pictured in 1962 was a 1949 Henschel, but had a new body built by Emmelman in 1960. Henschel built almost 700 trolley buses from 1941 until 1969, when it became a part of the Daimler-Benz organization. *Malcolm Chase*

The Kolner Verkehrs-Betriebe AG of Koln (Cologne), Germany, operated a very small 3.6-kilometer trolley bus route between 1950 and 1959. There were four Henschel/Uerdingen trolley buses in the service. One of them is pictured here with a trailer. The other three trolley buses in the Koln fleet were also manufactured by Henschel, two with Kassbohrer bodywork and one with a body by Uerdingen. After the system closed in 1959, the trolley buses went into service elsewhere. *D. A. Jones London Trolley Bus Preservation Society*

Pictured is a Henschel/Kassbohrer trolley bus built in 1947 for the Bremerhaven, Germany, trolley bus system. Two of these trolley buses were acquired by the Stadtwerke Hildesheim, Germany, system in 1952. The Hildesheim trolley bus system actually began in 1943 with five Henschel/Schumann trolley buses. Additional Henschel trolley buses with various bodies also entered service in Hildesheim. There was even one Italian-built three-axle Breda in the fleet. Eight of the early Henschel trolley buses were also three-axle models. *D. A. Jones London Trolley Bus Preservation Society*

The Stadtwerke Rheydt (Germany) operated a trolley bus service between 1953 and 1973. There were two routes totaling 28 kilometers with 15 trolley buses. Pictured is a Mercedes-Benz O 6600T trolley bus built in 1952. This vehicle originally served as a demonstrator in Buenos Aires, Argentina. Buenos Aires eventually bought 700 trolley buses, including 350 of this model. After its service in Buenos Aires, this trolley bus was in the Rheydt fleet between 1957 and 1970. In 1974, a year after trolley bus service ended, the city of Rheydt was annexed by neighboring Monchengladbach and the municipal transport authority lost its identity. *D. A. Jones London Trolley Bus Preservation Society*

The Stadtwerke Osnabruck Verkehrsbetriebe in Osnabruck, Germany, began operating a trolley bus service in 1949, initially to complement, and later to replace, an existing tramway network. There were 17 single-deck and 18 deck-and-a-half trolley buses in the fleet. The trolley bus pictured was acquired in 1953. It was built by Henschel in 1947 and was first operated in Kiel, Germany. When it came to Osnabruck it was rebodied by FAKA. When the Osnabruck trolley bus system ended in 1968, 20 of the vehicles were converted to motor buses. Another seven trolley bus bodies were transplanted to rebody existing motor buses. Only eight Osnabruck trolley buses were scrapped. *D. A. Jones London Trolley Bus Preservation Society*

Neuss, Germany, a city located on the Rhine River opposite Dusseldorf, had a small trolley bus system beginning in 1948. It had one 9.5-kilometer route with two branches linking the city center with a residential district. Five Henschel/Kassbohrer trolley buses, one of which is pictured here, were in the initial fleet. There were also two 1955 4-axle Henschel articulated trolley buses in service in Neuss. The system was operated by the Stadtwerke Neuss Abteilung Verkehrsbetriebe and closed in 1960. *D. A. Jones London Trolley Bus Preservation Society*

The Berlin, Germany, trolley bus system began in 1933. After World War II, when the service was in West Berlin, the Berliner Verkehrsbetriebe (BVG) operated it. This six-wheel Henschel/Kassbohrer trolley bus, one of two, began service in 1954. Three similar models were delivered in 1942. The trolley buses were discontinued in 1965. There was a separate system in East Berlin. Two short-lived trolley bus systems operated in Berlin in the early part of the 20th Century. *D. A. Jones London Trolley Bus Preservation Society*

One of the world's most interesting, and possibly the largest trolley bus, is shown here. It was built in 1955 by LOWA Werdau and LEW Henningsdorf for the Berliner Verkehrs-Betriebe (BVB) in East Berlin, Germany. The power unit in front had the trolley poles, which were raised and lowered pneumatically. The double-deck passenger trailer had 42 seats in the upper deck and 20 seats in the lower deck. It is reported the vehicle was little used. There were eight similar vehicles but their power unit had a diesel engine. *D. A. Jones London Trolley Bus Preservation Society*

Dresden, Germany, first opened a trolley bus line in 1947. It reached a maximum extension of 17 kilometers in 1964. The picture shows one of 30 Czech-built Skoda 9 Tr trolley buses delivered to Dresden between 1962 and 1964. LOWA in Bautzen, Germany, built the drawbar trailers. The Dresden trolley bus system ended in 1975. Some of its Skoda trolley buses saw service in Potsdam, Gera, and Eberswalde, Germany. Dresden also had a five-vehicle trolley bus system for two years, from 1903 to 1905.

Solingen, Germany, has had a trolley bus system since 1952 and it continues. In 1986-1987, 46 MAN Model SL 172HO three-axle trolley buses were acquired. One of these is pictured here. Solingen has been a source of used trolley buses for Sarajevo, Bosnia, and Mendoza, Argentina. *Wilhelm Pflug*

Essen (Germany) Verkehrs-AG (EVAG) operated the only guided trolley bus system in Germany, but it was short-lived. Pictured here is one of the 18 Mercedes-Benz Model 0 405 GGTD duobuses delivered to Essen in 1986/87. The trolley buses operated in a tunnel leaving the main railway station, then on a guided roadway. The electric mode was discontinued in 1995, but diesel buses operate the route today. *Wilhelm Pflug*

Esslingen-Nellingon Denkendof Verkehrsgesellschaft in Esslingen, Germany, continues to operate a trolley bus system that began in 1944. Pictured is one of the 18 Mercedes-Benz Model 0 405 GTD dual-mode trolley buses. It was delivered in 1994. Esslingen trolley buses operate under wire in the center of the city, but change to diesel power in the outer areas.

On the 50th anniversary of trolley buses in Solingen, Germany, in 2002, the Stadtwerke Solingen GmbH acquired 10 Van Hool AG300T trolley buses, one of which is pictured here. In 2000 Solingen received 16 Berkhof Premier AT18 trolley buses. These 21st Century trolley buses are the first non-German trolley buses to enter the Solingen fleet. The Berkhof trolley buses are manufactured in the Netherlands, and the Van Hools in are built in Belgium. *Van Hool*

Pictured is one of five Austrian-built Graf & Stift Model NGT 204 M 16. 5 low-floor articulated buses with Kiepe electric that entered service in Eberswalde, Germany, in 1994. Trolley bus service began in Eberswalde in 1940 and continues. The city also had a short-lived, single-vehicle trolley bus operating for three months in 1901. The Eberswalde system had a number of Ikarus 280 93T trolley buses when the area was East Germany.

When Berlin, Germany, was divided, the East Berlin system was known as the Berliner Verkehrs-Betriebe (BVB). It had trolley bus service between 1951 and 1973. The first 46 BVB trolley buses were built at LOWA factories in Werdau and Ammendorf, Germany. The trolley bus pictured is the W 602 type and was built in 1954. LOWA also built passenger trailers. *D. A. Jones London Trolley Bus Preservation Society*

The city of Offenbach, Germany, which borders Frankfurt on the east, began replacing a tramway network with trolley buses in 1951. By 1955 the trolley bus network had reached 15 kilometers and remained that size for 10 years. There were 41 trolley buses representing a variety of types in the fleet. Pictured is a Mercedes-Benz Model OE 6600 demonstrator of 1955, which operated until 1970. The system began closing in 1966 and the last trolley buses ran in Offenbach in 1972. *D. A. Jones London Trolley Bus Preservation Society*

Kreis Moerser Verkehrsbetriebe operated a number of interurban trolley bus routes in Moers, Germany, beginning in 1950. Moers is located on the Rhine River. The trolley bus routes replaced worn out interurban tramway networks of different gauges. The longest route was a distance of 30 kilometers, and the schedule took 74 minutes. One route crossed the Rhine and was a joint service with the Duisburger Verkehrsgesellschaft. There were 45 trolley buses, not all at one time, plus 14 drawbar trailers. The Moers trolley bus pictured is one of the 13 Bussing/Uerdingen Model UB IV vehicles that entered service in the late 1950s. Trolley bus service in the Moers area ended in 1968. *D. A. Jones London Trolley Bus Preservation Society*

Stadtwerke Solingen (Germany) GmbH didn't begin trolley bus service until 1952 and was the 64th of 69 German cities with modern trolley bus systems. Henschel/Uerdingen built the initial trolley buses, one of which is pictured here. This model, the Model UH111, was a very common trolley bus in Germany. It entered the Solingen fleet in 1959 and was withdrawn from service after 697,046 kilometers in 1965. *Wilhelm Pflug*

## Netherlands

Three cities in the Netherlands had trolley bus systems. One of the earliest systems was established in 1927 in Groningen, with equipment from Britain. Those original trolley buses were rebodied in the Netherlands in the late 1940s and continued in service until 1965, when the system closed.

Trolley bus service was established in Arnhem in 1949. Both the towns of Arnhem and Nijmegen acquired British trolley bus chassis with bodies that were constructed in the Netherlands. Only Arnhem has continued to operate trolley buses. The town is proud of its distinction, with its vehicles proclaiming "Arnhem Trolleystad" (Arnhem Trolley Town). The trolley bus system in Arnhem now operates as a part of a regional bus company. Articulated dual-mode vehicles for both city and suburban routes have replaced two-axle trolley buses on short town routes. The Nijmegen system began in 1952 and was discontinued in 1969.

This interesting view shows Groningen, Netherlands, No. 1 trolley bus in 1927 operating in an unusual manner. Although Groningen had trams, there was no trolley bus wiring to the tram depot where the trolley buses were housed. Therefore, the trolley buses were powered using one pole attached to the overhead tram wire and the other pole connected with a cable to a skate on the tram track, a procedure that had to be performed carefully. There were six trolley buses like this one, built by Daimler in England. They ran until 1951 when they were rebuilt with Verheul bodies. *Jan Voerman*

The trolley bus system in Groningen, Netherlands, began in 1927, and was the first in that country. The Daimler Co., Ltd. in Coventry built the original six trolley buses in England. Two had bodies from Vickers in England and the other four had locally built bodies by Woest. Bull Motors, Ltd. provided the motors. This picture, taken May 26, 1944, shows trolley bus No. 1 on a special trip for tram enthusiasts at the terminus at Kraneweg. Note the masked headlights used during World War II. *Jan Voerman*

In 1949 Gemeentelijk Vervoerbedrijf in Groningen, Netherlands, bought its first new trolley buses in 22 years. The city acquired ten 29-passenger trolley buses from Kromhout Motoren Fabriek, which built them in the Netherlands. They were the only trolley buses built by the company. One of the 10 Kromhout trolley buses, with Verheul body, is pictured. They operated in Groningen for 10 years, until the system closed in 1965. *Jan Voerman*

After the original six trolley buses in Groningen, Netherlands, had served more than 20 years, the Gemeentelijk Vervoerbedrijf decided to give these trolley buses new life with new bodies. In 1951 Auto-Industrie Verheul, an important Dutch bus body builder, rebodied the old trolley buses. Pictured is one of the Groningen trolley buses with a new 25-passenger body. These trolley buses saw service until 1958. *Jan Voerman*

Gemeente Vervoerbedrijf Arnhem (GVA), in Arnhem, Netherlands, began adding a new generation of trolley buses in 1980 and continued to do so through 1987. These new trolley buses were known as the B7900 type. Den Oudsten of Woerden, Netherlands, a bus manufacturer, built 41 of these trolley buses with DAF running parts for Arnhem service. The trolley bus pictured went out of service in 1982-1983 and was used for testing alternative propulsion in the form of a flywheel in 1996.

This Berkhof Model Premier AT 1B trolley bus and 21 similar ones are operating for the Gemeente Vervoerbedrijf in Arnhem, Netherlands. Delivery was made over five years beginning in 1993. These trolley buses are articulated low-floor models. A Deutz air-cooled diesel engine powers a 660 V generator, which acts as auxiliary power when the trolley bus cannot operate under wire. Berkhof didn't begin building trolley buses until this order was received. Solingen, Germany, received six similar Berkhof trolley buses at the same time. *Bill McDonald*

Van Hool of Koningshooikt, Belgium, has been a major builder of buses since 1947. Their products have been exported in large numbers to many parts of the world. The company did not build trolley buses until 1984, when it supplied Ghent, Belgium, with its first trolley buses. In 1993, nine Van Hool Model AG300T trolley buses were delivered to the Gemeente Vervoerbedrijf Arnhem in the Netherlands. One of these trolley buses is pictured leaving the Arnhem Central Station. The large contractor Connexxion now operates the system.

Arnhem, Netherlands, lost most of its transit system in the World War II battle of Arnhem in September 1944. Rather than rebuild the tram system, it was decided to restart the system with trolley buses. The first route was opened in 1949. Initially, 36 new trolley buses were ordered from BUT in England. The Dutch bus body builder Verheul built bodies for these trolley buses. Two of the first trolley buses for Arnhem are pictured. *Jan Voerman*

Pictured is one of the seven second-generation trolley buses that entered service in 1955/56 for the Gemeente Vervoerbedrijf in Arnhem, Netherlands. They served for more than 20 years. They were built by BUT in England but bodied by Verheul in the Netherlands. These trolley buses had seating for 37 passengers. In the mid-1960s, when these trolley buses were operating, there were 43 trolley buses in service in Arnhem. *Jan Voerman*

Nijmegen, Netherlands, began a trolley bus system in 1952 with 14 BUT 9721T trolley buses with bodies by the Dutch manufacturer Auto-Industrie Verheul in Waddinxveen. Pictured is the first Nijmegen trolley bus. Only six more trolley buses were acquired for service in Nijmegen and were added in 1957. They were similar to the first 14 trolley buses and were built by BUT with Verheul bodies. *Jan Voerman*

## Switzerland

Trams dominated in many cities in Switzerland, but Lausanne developed a substantial trolley bus network beginning in 1932. It was the first major trolley bus system in Switzerland and continues to be the largest.

The popularity of the trolley bus in Switzerland may be due to a ready supply of cheap electricity, strong public awareness of environmental concerns, and a hilly terrain. High-quality maintenance and careful refurbishment have ensured long-lasting vehicles, with some in Lausanne achieving almost 50 years of use.

Fourteen trolley bus systems continue to operate in Switzerland. Basel, one of Switzerland's largest cities, has one of the smallest trolley bus fleets, and there are some signs the trolley buses will be eliminated. Several medium-sized cities, such as Biel, Neuchatel, and Winterthur, have significant systems with new vehicles.

Switzerland also had a number of scenic rural and intercity trolley bus systems. In Thun a system began in 1952. It operated for some distance along Lake Thun and was one of the most picturesque trolley bus systems in the world. Another interesting trolley bus service was the one operated in the Val-de-Ruz area, which connected several small communities near Neuchatel and at one time even connected with the Neuchatel system. In Altstatten a trolley bus system operated from 1940 to 1977 and had rural routes. All three of these rural systems have closed. The system in Montreux-Vevey operates on a route near the north side of Lake Geneva, connecting a number of close-knit communities on the route.

In addition to having many trolley bus systems, manufacturers in Switzerland, such as Saurer, FBW, Berna, and Hess, produced most of the trolley buses for that country. Secheron, a world electrical company, has been important in supplying electrical equipment for trolley buses for many years. It was founded in Geneva.

A new development has been the use of biarticulated trolley buses in Geneva. The system was introduced recently and operates some of the only biarticulated trolley buses in the world.

Compagnie des Transports au Val-de-Ruz of Cernier, Switzerland, operated trolley buses on a picturesque 14.4-km rural route between Les Hauts-Geneveys and Villiers. It began in 1948 and closed in 1984. Pictured is a Saurer trolley bus of 1942, but with a body rebuilt in the late 1960s. The fleet was very small, with a maximum of eight trolley buses operating at one time. The Val-de-Ruz trolley buses were seen pulling trailers on some of the schedules.

Societe Electrique Vevey-Montreux (Switzerland) did not begin operating trolley buses until 1957, after 16 other trolley bus systems had been established in Switzerland. The first vehicles were 18 trolley buses built by the Swiss firm Berna in 1940. One of the Berna trolley buses is pictured with the Chateau de Chillon on the shores of Lake Geneva in the background. The system continues with newer Van Hool trolley buses.

Switzerland's first city trolley bus operation began in 1932 in Lausanne. It has also been the largest system in that country. Swiss firms have built most of the trolley buses in Switzerland. FBW (Franz Brozincevic & Wetzikon), Wetzikon, Switzerland, was one of the early trolley bus builders, and 32 of these FBW trolley buses with Eggli bodies went into service for the Societe des Tramways Lausannois in 1937. These were the only ones of this type built. *Wilhelm Pflug*

Societe d'Tramways de Fribourg (Switzerland), now Transports en commun de Fribourg, began operating trolley buses in 1949, and the system continues today. The first Fribourg trolley buses were built in France by Societe des Vehicules et Tracteurs Electriques (Vetra). Eight Model VCR Vetras were delivered to Fribourg in 1948. One of the early ones is pictured here. The modern Fribourg trolley buses were built by Volvo and have Hess bodies. *Malcolm Chase*

The Stadt Verkehrsbetriebe Bern (Switzerland) began operating trolley buses in 1941. Two of the first trolley buses in Bern were these Model T 51 vehicles built by Franz Brozincevic & Wetzikon (FBW). They were pictured in 1945. FBW built more than 500 trolley buses between 1941 and 1984. All but six FBW trolley buses were acquired by Swiss trolley bus operations. The six that were exported went to Bratislava, Slovakia. Trolley bus service continues in Bern with about 44 articulated units.

Switzerland has been the scene of considerable trolley bus interest, including several interurban services. The Steffisburg-Thun-Interlaken company operated a notable interurban trolley bus line that replaced a tramway between Thun and Beatenbucht. Nine Berna trolley buses with Gangloff bodies went into service in 1952. One of the Berna trolley buses with a trailer is seen traveling along the shores of Lake Thun. Buses replaced the nine trolley buses in 1982.

Motorwagenfabrik Berna AG, Olten, Switzerland, had its beginnings in 1910. In 1929 the Swiss firm Saurer took controlling interest in Berna, but kept it as a separate identity. The first Berna trolley buses were built in 1940. That same year Stadtische Verkehrsbetriebe Biel (Switzerland) acquired its first trolley buses from Berna. Pictured is a 1949 Berna trolley bus that operated for many years in Biel. It had a Hess body. *Malcolm Chase*

Franz Brozincevic & Wetzikon (FBW), Wetzikon, Switzerland, began building trucks in 1910. The company built its first bus in 1926 and its first trolley bus in 1932. A total of 521 trolley buses were built prior to 1960. Most popular was the Model T 51, and 198 of these were built. One of the 12 T 51 trolley buses that went into service in 1955 for the Basler Verkehrs-Betriebe in Basel, Switzerland, is shown here. The Basel FBW T 51 trolley buses ran for more than 30 years. *Malcolm Chase*

In the 1950s there were experiments and actual transportation services operated with gyrobuses. The gyrobus had a flywheel that was charged about every five kilometers. Three poles from the top of the gyrobus would be extended at the stations and the flywheel would be charged. The gyrobus was not a trolley bus, but it had similarities. It was developed by the Swiss firm Maschinenfabrik Oerlikon. Ten systems operated gyrobuses, the most notable one in Yverdon, Switzerland. It operated from 1950 to 1960. One of the Yverdon gyrobuses is pictured in Yverdon. Others operated in Kinshasa, Zaire, and in Ghent-Merelboke, Belgium. On occasion, the use of flywheels for powering buses has been considered in various cities.

This Saurer trolley bus with a Hess body is one of seven that first entered the service of Verkehrsbetriebe der Stadt Winterthur, Winterthur, Switzerland, in 1960. It served for more than 30 years in Winterthur. Trolley bus service began in Winterthur in 1938 and continues with approximately 53 trolley buses. The Adolph Saurer Company was an important Swiss vehicle manufacturer from 1903. The first Saurer trolley bus was built in 1932.

Geneva, Switzerland, has had trolley bus service since 1942 and it continues today. Pictured is one of the 21 Berna trolley buses acquired in 1965. These trolley buses had Ramsier & Jenzer bodies. In 1963 Compagnie Genevoise des Tramways Electriques, operator of the Geneva system, had 66 trolley buses in the fleet. Transports Publics Genevoise, which currently operates transit in Geneva, has 73 trolley buses in its fleet.

The Verkehrsbetriebe der Stadt Luzern (VBL), Luzern, Switzerland, bought 14 of these articulated Model 13R trolley buses from the German firm Bussing in 1965/66. These were the first and only Bussing trolley buses to operate in Switzerland. They ran in Luzern service until 1988. Trolley buses began operating in Luzern in 1941 and the service continues today.

Verkehrsbetriebe der Stadt St. Gallen, St. Gallen, Switzerland, began trolley bus service in 1950 and it continues today. This trolley bus, pictured in St. Gallen in 1968, was originally built in 1950 by Saurer, but was rebodied by Hess in 1968. It is seen towing a passenger trailer, which was common in Switzerland at the time. The St. Gallen system now has approximately 63 trolley buses. *Malcolm Chase*

Trolley bus service began in La Chaux-de-Fonds, Switzerland, in 1949 and continues to serve the community. The Saurer/Secheron trolley bus pictured is one of four that were originally in service in Geneva, Switzerland, beginning in 1942. La Chaux-de-Fonds acquired them in 1974-1976. Later they were refurbished and received Haag-built bodies. Compagne des Transports en Commune now operates the La Chaux-de-Fonds trolley bus service.

The Stadtische Verkehrsbetriebe Biel (VB), in Biel, Switzerland, began operating trolley buses in 1946 and the service continues. The Swiss firm Berna built the first Biel trolley buses. Pictured is one of the six Ramsier & Jenzer-bodied Volvo articulated trolley buses that first entered service in 1986. The Biel system has four trolley bus routes.

Verkehrsbetriebe der Stadt Zurich (VBZ) in Zurich, Switzerland, began operating trolley buses in 1939 and the service continues to operate today. Swiss-built FBW trolley buses were the first choice for Zurich trolley buses and continued for almost 20 years. This Model 91GTL articulated trolley bus along with 30 others was from FBW. It came to Zurich in 1974 and served on the trolley bus routes for many years.

Compagnie des Tramways de Neuchatel (Switzerland) has had a trolley bus system since 1940. In 1964-1965, 20 Saurer Model 4TP54 trolley buses were acquired. One is seen here pulling a passenger trailer, which has been common for Swiss trolley bus systems. Neuchatel turned to FBW trolley buses in 1976, when 20 were purchased. The Neuchatel system is now Transports Publics du Littoral Neuchatelois.

This Mercedes-Benz Model 0405 6TZ trolley bus was delivered to the Verkehrsbetriebe der Stadt Zurich (VBZ), in Zurich, Switzerland, in 1989. It was one of 36 similar trolley buses for Zurich. This model is interesting because it has a rear-mounted electric motor for the rear axle and a diesel engine in the front section, and transmits power to the center axle by angular gears. It is effective for operating on winter roads. The Zurich system began in 1939 and continues with a fleet of about 80 trolley buses.

Basler Verkehrs-Betriebe (BVB), Basel, Switzerland, is one of the 14 trolley bus operators in Switzerland today. The Basel trolley bus system was never large, and there are only 12 Neoplan Model N6020 articulated trolley buses in the current Basel fleet. They were all acquired in 1992. Basel trolley bus service began in 1941.

VMCV Transports Publics is the name of the transportation system serving the Swiss cities of Vevey, Montreux, Clarens, and Villeneuve, along the north shore of Lake Geneva. In 1993, 18 Van Hool Model AG300T trolley buses, one of which is pictured here, went into service. Trolley buses first began serving the area cities in 1957.

Trolley buses have been important in Geneva, Switzerland, since 1942. Over the years the trolley bus service in Geneva has been a progressive system with some of the newest trolley buses. In early 2004 a 24-meter articulated trolley bus was introduced. The Swiss firm Carroceria Hess in Bellach built it. Geneva has been receiving 38 articulated trolley buses from Hess and 10 double-articulated trolley buses are being added. One is pictured here. It has Vossloh Kiepe electrics.

In 1999, Neoplan, Stuttgart, Germany, began delivering 27 of its Model N6121 low-floor, articulated trolley buses to Transports Publics de la Region Lausannoise, Lausanne, Switzerland. The new trolley buses are painted overall white with blue trim and have spats over the wheels of the second and third axles. These trolley buses proved unsatisfactory and are no longer in service in Lausanne.

Transports Regionalaux Neuchatelois, which now operates urban transportation in La Chaux-de-Fonds, Switzerland, has new Solaris trolley buses in service. They were acquired in 2005. There are three Model 12AC Trollino rigid trolley buses and four new Model 18AC articulated trolley buses in the fleet. One of the 12AC trolley buses is pictured. *Peter Blears Collection*

Stadtbus Winterthur (Switzerland) began taking delivery of 10 Polish-built Solaris Trollino 18AC articulated trolley buses in 2005. The first of these new trolley buses is pictured. Winterthur began trolley bus service in 1938. The Swiss firm Saurer built the first Winterthur trolley buses. Only Swiss-built trolley buses were acquired by Winterthur until 1989 when 14 Mercedes-Benz 0 405 trolley buses entered the fleet. *Bill MacDonald*

The Nottingham (England) Corporation Passenger Transport Department had one of the early British trolley bus systems, beginning in 1927. The system had 10 of the 110 trolley buses that were built between 1913 and 1926 by the Railless firm in London. It was one of the pioneer trolley bus types with rubber tires and a single tram-like headlight. One of these trolley buses is pictured here. Nottingham continued its fairly large trolley bus system until 1966. The Nottingham area also had another trolley bus system operated by the Nottinghamshire and Derbyshire Traction Co. between 1932 and 1953. *G. H. F. Atkins©/Courtesy of the John Banks Collection*

## *United Kingdom*

The United Kingdom has an important place in trolley bus history. The British adopted trolley bus technology somewhat later than elsewhere, and were able to avoid some of the mistakes made by others, resulting in vehicles that were fairly reliable. Although the United Kingdom was not a pioneer in trolley bus technology, it made its mark as a developer, large-scale operator, and manufacturer.

A number of trolley bus systems in Britain began in the early 1900s as extensions of trams. Several British systems survived World War I. After the war, fleets needed renewal and several manufacturers entered the market and developed new designs. These new designs helped make the trolley bus attractive to towns operating old-fashioned or worn-out trams or street cars.

Most of the trolley buses in service in Britain were double-deck vehicles. The British influence on the trolley bus was strong, not only throughout the British Empire and its colonies, but also elsewhere in the world. Britain was not just a source of chassis and bodies, but also influenced the use of double-deck trolley buses, as in Australia and South Africa.

The nationalization of electricity undermined the economics of many trolley bus systems, so that after 1950 motor buses rather than trolley buses replaced most of the remaining street car routes or systems.

The trolley bus system in London was large, with more than 1,800 vehicles in service at one point. In 1962 it became one of the world's first large systems to close. Other large systems were in Wolverhampton, Belfast, Bradford, Glasgow, and Newcastle Upon Tyne. Rotherham began a trolley bus system in 1912, which continued until 1965. The Mexborough & Swinton Traction Co. Ltd. in Rotherham began in 1915 and lasted until 1961. The system in Teesside began in 1919 and ended in 1971. The Bradford system was very significant. It operated from 1911 until 1972, and was the last trolley bus service in Britain.

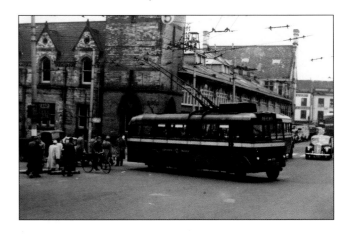

The County Borough of Darlington (England) Transport Department replaced its tram system with trolley buses in early 1926. Pictured is one of the 24 Model W trolley buses operated in Darlington. They were built by Karrier Motors Ltd. of Luton, England, with Brush Electrical Engineering Co. bodies. Except for six British United Traction Ltd. double-deck trolley buses delivered in 1949, all the Darlington trolley buses were single-deck models. Most of the Darlington Karrier single-deck trolley buses went to Bradford where they received new double-deck bodies. Trolley bus service ended in Darlington in 1957.

There were many manufacturers of trolley buses in Britain. In the early days Ransomes, Sims & Jefferies, Ltd. was an important builder of British trolley buses. Sunbeam Trolleybus Co. came later, as well as British United Traction Co. These two companies also exported many trolley buses. Leyland Motors and Associated Equipment Co. (AEC) were also important in building trolley buses, but mostly for the domestic market. One of the world's leading manufacturers of motors and electrical equipment for trolley buses was the Metropolitan-Vickers Co. It supplied equipment not only for Britain, but also for many other countries. Other electrical firms were British Thompson-Houston Co., Compton Parkinson Ltd., and English Electric Co.

British trolley buses that retained the half-cab and exposed radiator layout of contemporary motor buses were often referred to as "the Diddlers." (One was "diddled" or deceived into believing that the vehicle was a motor bus.) The fact that one of these vehicles sweeping up to a bus stop would betray no internal combustion engine noise would tell most people that here was something new, but six-cylinder gasoline engines were smooth and silent and perhaps it was easy to be deceived. There was, in fact, no reason at all why a trolley bus should not have had a radiator grille air intake; electrical equipment also needed cooling. Pictured is No. 1 in the Birmingham (England) Corporation fleet, a 1932 Short Bros-bodied Leyland TBD1. A 48-seater, it ran until 1940. *G. H. F. Atkins©/Courtesy of the John Banks Collection*

Trolley bus service was inaugurated in the pleasant and popular resort of Bournemouth, England, in 1933 by the Bournemouth Corporation Transport. When trams operated the Christchurch route, at the end of the line the trams were reversed for the return trip. When trolley buses replaced the trams a turntable had to be installed in a dead-end alley to turn the trolley buses around. When a trolley bus was on the turntable, a crew pushed on it until it was heading in the return direction. In this picture a couple of small boys delighted in helping. The trolley bus shown, No. 303, was a Sunbeam Model MF 2B with Weymann bodywork, and was the last of nine delivered to Bournemouth. Interestingly, this trolley bus was the last one built in Great Britain that operated in regular service. *Loring M. Lawrence*

Derby (England) Corporation Transport began operating a trolley bus system in January 1932. It continued until September 1957. The first Derby trolley buses were 20 Guy Motors BTX vehicles. Six had bodies by the Brush Electrical Engineering Co., Ltd., Loughborough, and 14 were bodied by Christopher Dodson of Willesden in northwest London. Dodson was better known as the provider of bodywork for the main independent operators in London. Derby's No. 83 was a Brush-bodied example with, despite the three-axled chassis, only 56 seats. The vehicle was fitted with a Rees Roturbo 75-hp motor and was photographed in July 1932 at Market Place, Derby. Trolley buses had less chance of further service when sold by their first owner than did motor buses, although such use was not unknown. This one had no such good fortune and was withdrawn in 1949 and scrapped. *G. H. F. Atkins©/Courtesy of the John Banks Collection*

The English town of Chesterfield, Derbyshire, had one of the shortest-lived trolley bus systems in Britain. Opened in 1927 by the Chesterfield Corporation Transport, it was, despite its success, abandoned in 1938. The first vehicles, delivered from April through July 1927, were single-deck 32-seaters with a BTH 60-hp motor and center-entrance bodywork by Reeve & Kenning. Straker-Clough built the chassis. Note in the picture the unusual "one over the other" arrangement of trolley poles. There were 15 of these vehicles. No. 14 is illustrated in a March 1934 photograph at Sephenson Place, Chesterfield. *G. H. F. Atkins©/Courtesy of the John Banks Collection*

The London (England) Passenger Transport Board had one of the world's largest trolley bus systems. It began in 1931 and continued until 1962. The service was quite extensive with 68 routes, some of them quite long, and more than 1,800 trolley buses. Most of London's trolley buses, except for a few experimental models, were 70-passenger, six-wheel vehicles. Pictured is one of the typical London trolley buses. The Associated Equipment Co. (AEC) built it in 1938 with a Metropolitan-Cammell Carriage & Wagon body. Leyland Motors also built many of the London trolley buses. When trolley bus service was phased out in the late 1950s and 1960s, many of the London double-deck trolley buses went into service in Spain. *Peter Blears Collection*

The Associated Equipment Co., Ltd. (AEC) delivered 44 of these 54-seat, double-deck trolley buses to the Brighton (England) Corporation Transport in 1939, the year the system began. They had Weymann bodies and motors by Compton Parkinson Ltd. The Brighton Hove & District Co., Ltd., a private area transport company, shared the trolley bus system with the Brighton Corporation. It paid for the use of the Brighton trolley bus overhead and provided a portion of the trolley bus fleet. This private company began trolley bus service in 1946 and ended service in 1959. Brighton Corporation trolley buses operated for two more years. *Peter Blears Collection*

Wales had five trolley bus systems, although not all were in operation at the same time. The largest system served the Welsh capital city, Cardiff, from 1942 until 1970. It was operated by the Cardiff Corporation Transport Department. There were 79 maroon-and-cream trolley buses on 14 routes covering 18 miles. Because of low clearance at a railway underpass, single-deck trolley buses were always on the Bute Street route. All other Cardiff trolley buses were double-deck vehicles. Pictured is one of 13 British United Traction Model 9641T trolley buses with bodywork by East Lancashire Coachbuilders. *Loring M. Lawrence*

The last Hastings Tramways Company trolley buses were delivered from 1946 through 1948. They were Sunbeam W models built to wartime austerity specifications. Number 33, which is pictured, was one of the 1947 arrivals. It had bodywork seating 56 built by the Addlestone, Surrey, coachbuilder Weymann's Motor Bodies Ltd. *G. H. F. Atkins©/Courtesy of the John Banks Collection*

Pictured is one of the 30 Sunbeam Trolleybus Company Model F4 trolley buses delivered to Derby, England, in 1948-1949. Each featured Brush Electrical Engineering bodies. Number 199 entered service in January 1949 and was withdrawn in 1966. A further 20 Sunbeam F4s joined the Derby Corporation Transport fleet in 1952-1953. Eight of the modified F4A versions were purchased in 1960. They were the last trolley buses bought by this operator. *G. H. F. Atkins©/Courtesy of the John Banks Collection*

The Bradford (England) City Transport began the first trolley bus service in Britain in 1911. It started with two Railless Electric Traction Co. vehicles. It was not a short-lived system, but continued for more than 60 years, finally closing down in 1972. It was the last trolley bus operation in Britain to close. Some of the Bradford trolley bus routes extended beyond the city boundaries. The area had some steep hill routes, maximizing the advantage of trolley buses. Pictured is one of the 10 Sunbeam Trolleybus Co., Ltd. Model MF2 trolley buses that entered service in 1942. These trolley buses had Weymann bodies that were rebuilt by East Lancashire Coachbuilders in 1956. *Peter Blears Collection*

London Transport's last and only postwar trolley buses were a large batch of British United Traction (a combined Leyland-AEC initiative formed to market trolley buses) 70 seaters, fitted with 8-foot-wide body-work by the Metropolitan Cammell Carriage & Wagon Company. New in 1948 through 1952, they were prematurely withdrawn and most were sold for further service in Spain, including No. 1795, which is pictured. This trolley bus went to the La Coruna (Corunna) Tramways Company in Spain. In happier times it is seen in London's suburb of Chiswick. *G. H. F. Atkins© /Courtesy of the John Banks Collection*

The Nottinghamshire and Der-byshire Traction Company of Nottingham, England, operated an interurban trolley bus system beginning in 1932. It had what was the longest trolley bus route in Britain, a distance of 16 miles through mining villages and up and down hills. The service entered Nottingham, a city with a large trolley bus system, by sharing overhead wires. Pictured is one of the 15 British Electric Traction Ltd. trolley buses that were acquired for operation on the interurban line in 1949. They had Weymanns Ltd. bodywork. The trolley buses ended their service in 1959 and were replaced with diesel buses. *Peter Blears Collection*

Glasgow had the only trolley bus system in Scotland except one in Dundee that began in 1912 and lasted only a year and a half. Glasgow Corporation Transport didn't begin service until 1949, but the system grew quickly to almost 200 trolley buses. One of the Glasgow trolley buses, a Sunbeam Trolleybus Co. Model F4 A, pictured here, was added to the fleet in 1953. It was one of 20 of this type. Although most Glasgow trolley buses were double-deck models, there were 10 single-deck trolley buses in the fleet. They were built by British Electric Traction Ltd. with Burlingham bodies. Trolley bus service ended in Glasgow in 1967. *Peter Blears Collection*

Reading (England) Corporation Transport began trolley bus operations in 1936 when trams were replaced. While there were four numbered trolley bus routes, short branches meant there were eight possible destinations. In the mid-1960s the fleet consisted of 44 trolley buses, all double deckers. Pictured is one of ten 1950 Sunbeam Trolleybus Co. Model S-7s with British Thompson-Houston motors that were delivered to Reading. They had Park Royal bodies. The Reading trolley bus system closed in 1968. *Loring M. Lawrence*

The Rotherham (England) Corporation Transport Department was the second oldest trolley bus operation in Great Britain. The service began in 1912 with Railless Electric Traction Co. single-deck trolley buses. The next year three more were added. Rotherham favored single-deck trolley buses. In 1949 and 1950 44 Daimler Model CTC6 and CTE6 six-wheel, single-deck trolley buses were purchased. One of these models, which had an East Lancashire body, is pictured. In 1956, 20 of these Daimler trolley buses were converted to double-deck vehicles with new Charles H. Roe, Ltd. bodies.

Every trolley bus system needs support vehicles commonly called tower wagons. The two tower wagons pictured were in service by the Reading (England) Corporation Transport. Commer Cars Ltd. built the tower wagon on the left in 1947. It had a crew cab and was called an Eagle Tower. It was also used as a towing vehicle. The tower wagon on the right was a 1937 Leland, originally with London Transport but acquired by Reading in 1964. When Reading trolley bus service ended it was used for light towing. *Photo: Loring M. Lawrence; caption material: R. D. H. Symons*

Belfast, Northern Ireland, had the only trolley bus operation in Ireland. It began in 1938 by the Belfast Corporation Transport Department. The system became quite large and at one time was the second-largest trolley bus system in Great Britain. Service began with eight trolley buses built by Crossley Motors, Ltd., Guy Motors, Ltd., Karrier Motors, Ltd., and Leyland Motors, Ltd. Pictured is one of the 24 red-and-cream British United Traction double-deck trolley buses acquired in 1950. They had Harkness Coach Builders Ltd. bodies and General Electric motors. Trolley bus service in Belfast ended in 1968 after 30 years. *Loring M. Lawrence*

Bradford (England) City Transport acquired 40 Associated Equipment Co. trolley buses in 1938. English Electric Co. built the bodies. One of these trolley buses was fitted with new bodywork, and is pictured in 1969 as it passed under a low railway bridge on Route 37 to Clayton. Bradford had a number of hilly routes; therefore, trolley buses served the area very efficiently from 1911 until 1972, the longest operating trolley bus service in England. *Loring M. Lawrence*

Great Britain has a rich trolley bus history. There were 48 cities with trolley buses. Manchester had one of the larger systems. It was operated by the Manchester Corporation Transport Department. The service began in 1938 with 28 Crossley Motors Ltd. TDD4 trolley buses. Pictured is one of the 62 British United Traction double-deck trolley buses delivered to Manchester in 1956. There were 189 trolley buses in service in Manchester at one time. The service closed in 1966. *John Banks Collection*

Huddersfield, England, is a very hilly city; therefore, it was well suited to trolley buses. The Huddersfield Corporation Transport began trolley bus service in 1933 with a large fleet. At one time approximately 140 trolley buses were in service. Pictured is one of 10 Sunbeam Trolleybus Company trolley buses that entered service in 1959. They had East Lancashire Ltd. bodies and Metropolitan-Vickers motors. Between 1950 and 1963, Charles H. Roe and East Lancashire rebodied 69 vehicles. The Huddersfield fleet also included British United Traction and Karrier trolley buses. Trolley bus service continued to operate in Huddersfield until 1968.

The Hastings Tramways Company ran trolley buses in the English county of Sussex from 1928 to 1957. Its first trolley buses were a batch of 38 Guy BTX60 vehicles with Rees Roturbo 60-hp compound-wound motors and 57-seat bodywork built by Christopher Dodson of Willesden in north-west London. The bodies were unusual for that date in having open tops, although perhaps not so strange when it is recalled that they operated in a seaside town. The bodies also had open staircases. One of them, No. 3, was retained long after the other 27 had gone to the scrap yard and is seen in 1956 working a seaside tourist service. *G. H. F. Atkins©/ Courtesy of the John Banks Collection*

Pictured is one of the 30 six-wheel, double-deck trolley buses that were purchased by the Nottingham (England) Corporation beginning in 1950. They were built by British United Traction Ltd. with Brush bodies. The Nottingham trolley bus service had its start in 1927. The first 10 vehicles were trolley buses built by the Railless Electric Traction Co. Other early Nottingham trolley buses were built by Ransomes, Sims & Jefferies, Ltd. There were also six trolley buses built by English Electric Co. The Nottingham trolley bus system closed in 1966. *Peter Blears Collection*

England's largest county is Yorkshire, split into East, West, and North Ridings. A notable West Riding trolley bus operator was the Mexborough & Swinton Traction Co., Ltd. whose system ran from 1915 to 1961. The last batch of trolley buses purchased, in August 1950, were three single-deck Sunbeam F4s fitted with BTH 209 AY3 95-hp compound-wound motors and Brush center-entrance 32-seat bodywork. The first of the three, No. 37, is seen negotiating a tight corner typical of much of the company's operating territory. This vehicle and its two companions went on after withdrawal in 1961 to have a second career in Bradford, where they were rebodied as double-deckers. They ran thus until Bradford's system (the last in Great Britain) closed down in 1972. Enthusiast groups acquired all three for preservation. *G. H. F. Atkins©/ Courtesy of the John Banks Collection*

# Northern Europe
## Norway

Bergen is the only city that operates trolley buses in Norway today. In recent years Bergen has imported trolley buses from a number of countries and currently has several new MAN/Neoplan articulated trolley buses.

Oslo used tram or light rail for its main routes. Most of its network of trolley bus routes was built during the 1940s. The system ended in 1968. Stavanger operated the smallest system in Norway from 1947 to 1963, with just five vehicles.

One very interesting system began in Drammen in 1909. It was one of the few early systems to survive to the late 1960s, and was the last trolley bus system to use single-pole current collection with a forked end and closely spaced wiring.

This trolley bus became a part of the Drammen (Norway) Kommunale Trikk trolley bus fleet in 1951. It was one of eight with a British chassis by Ransomes, Sims & Jefferies, Ltd., and a body by the Norwegian firm Larvik Karosserifabrikk AS. It was unusual because it had a single forked pole that connected to narrowly spaced overhead wires. The Drammen trolley bus system began in 1909 and ended in 1967.

Trolley bus service in Drammen, Norway, began in 1909 and was one of the few early systems that survived, serving for almost 60 years. The trolley bus pictured entered service in 1910. Max Schiemann & Co. built it. There were five other Schiemann trolley buses in the Drammen fleet. At first they had hard rubber tires. Later, these six vehicles were fitted with pneumatic tires as shown in this picture.

Oslo, Norway, was one of four Norwegian cities that operated a trolley bus system. The service in Oslo began in 1940 and continued to 1968. Strommens Vaerksted built all of the 72 trolley buses that were operated in Oslo, and most were delivered between 1947 and 1952. No further trolley buses were added after 1952.

Four cities in Norway have operated trolley buses. Of the four, Bergen was the last to begin service, in 1950, and is the only one that continues to operate trolley buses. The firm Strommens Vaerksted built the first Bergen trolley buses as gasoline-powered buses in 1941 during World War II. Shortly afterward, it was reported, one of these buses was sent to Leipzig, Germany. The bus pictured was found and returned to Bergen. Bergen Sporvei converted it and seven similar vehicles to trolley buses in 1950 to operate the first trolley bus service.

Bergen Sporvei, Bergen, Norway, unlike other Norwegian systems, continues to operate trolley buses. In 1973, 20 Skoda 9 Tr trolley buses were imported from the Czechoslovakia firm. One of these trolley buses is pictured with the colorful Bryggen background. *O. Iskov*

This Volvo Model B58 trolley bus with a Swiss Hess body went into service in Bergen, Norway, in 1978, along with three others. Volvo also produced trolley buses for several Swiss cities and three cities in Italy, as well as supplying several trolley buses to Arnhem, Netherlands, and Wellington, New Zealand.

Even though it is a small system, the trolley bus system in Bergen, Norway, adds new trolley buses periodically. In 1980 three articulated Austrian-built Graf & Stift Model GE 17OM18 trolley buses were delivered and went into service in Bergen. They also carried a MAN badge on the front because Graf & Stift had become a subsidiary of the German firm MAN.

Modernization of the trolley bus fleet in Bergen, Norway, came in 2003, when six low-floor articulated MAN Model N6221G vehicles were acquired, one of which is pictured here. They had MAN chassis and Neoplan bodies. The Bergen trolley bus system began in 1950 and was operated by A/S Bergen Sporvei. The system is now part of a group of urban and suburban companies called Gaia Trafikk that trades under the name Bergen Buss.

## Denmark

Denmark, with its lack of hills and lack of coal or hydroelectricity for cheap power, is not ideally suited for trolley buses. However, the Nordsjaelland Elektricitats og Sporvejs Aktieselskab (NESA) system, based in the northern Copenhagen suburb of Hellerup, was an early installation that outlived other trolley bus systems in Denmark, operating from 1927 to 1971. Two routes were operated jointly by Kopenhavns Sporveje and NESA, an unusual situation for trolley bus operations. In 1993 an experimental route was opened in Copenhagen. It used the world's first duobuses, which operated both as a trolley bus and a diesel motor bus.

Odense (Denmark) Sporvej operated trolley buses for 20 years, between 1939 and 1959. The AEC trolley bus pictured had a Deforende Automobilfabriher (DFA Triangle) body and English Electric Company electrical equipment. It was placed in service in 1938 and withdrawn in 1959 when trolley bus service ended in Odense.

The Nordsjaelland Elektricitats og Sporvejs Aktieselskab (NESA) was a suburban trolley bus service in the Copenhagen, Denmark, area beginning in 1927. This trolley bus, which went into service in 1942, had a Scania chassis and a Frederiksborg Karrosefabrik body. It ran in regular service until 1962. The NESA trolley bus system closed in 1971.

Denmark had three trolley bus systems, the first of which was operated by NESA of Hellerup, beginning in 1927. Kopenhavns Sporveje in Copenhagen began its trolley bus system in 1938. Pictured is one of 13 British United Traction (BUT) LETB 1 trolley buses delivered in 1950. They had bodies by DAB (Dansk Automobil Byggeri) and served for 14 years. This trolley bus service ended in 1963. In 1993 trolley bus service returned to Copenhagen with the Hovedstradsomadets Trafikselskab (HT) operating Mercedes-Benz duobuses, but it was discontinued in 1997.

## Sweden

Sweden's newest trolley bus system is located in the small town of Landskrona. It began in 2003 with three trolley buses built by the Polish firm Solaris Bus & Coach. Sweden had only two other trolley bus systems, in Goteborg and Stockholm. Both ceased operations in 1964 when the rule of the road changed. The Stockholm system was quite large and operated some of the first articulated Alfa Romeo trolley buses. They were the only ones designed for left-hand rule of the road.

Sweden's two large bus and truck builders, Volvo and Scania, have built many trolley buses. When Stockholm and Goteborg had trolley bus systems most of the vehicles were built by Scania. Scania has also built trolley buses for Sao Paulo, Brazil. No Volvo trolley buses were in service in Sweden, but many Volvo trolley buses have operated in many world cities. Currently Volvo has a joint venture to produce trolley buses in China.

Goteborgs Sparvagar, in Goteborg, was the first trolley bus system in Sweden. It began in 1940 with 10 Lindholmen-built trolley buses. The tenth one is pictured here. They were followed a few years later by nine Scania Vabis trolley buses. Those 19 trolley buses were the only ones that operated in Goteborg. Trolley bus service ended in 1964, when Sweden's rule of the road changed.

Between 1947 and 1951, 112 Scania Vabis Model T-31 trolley buses went into service in Stockholm, Sweden, for the Stockholms Sparvagar. Trolley bus service began in Stockholm in 1941 and ended in 1964 when the Swedish rule of the road was changed. Pictured in 1949 is one of the 112 Scania Vabis trolley buses. The first 70 trolley buses to enter service in Stockholm were also built by Scania Vabis. The Stockholm system's largest fleet of trolley buses was in 1951-1952 with 189 vehicles. *Lennart Welander*

This trolley bus, one of 10, was delivered to the Atkiebolaget Stockholms Sparvagar in Stockholm, Sweden, in 1950. These Alfa Romeo Model 140 AFS trolley buses were the only ones of this type built, and are said to be the first articulated trolley buses to operate in Europe. These trolley buses were also unusual because they had four axles. At the time, Sweden's rule of the road was on the left; therefore, the extra-wide doors were on the left side of the vehicles. Trolley bus service began in Stockholm in 1941 and ended in 1964. *Lennart Welander*

The only trolley buses currently operating in Sweden are in Landskrona. It is a new system that began in September 2003. Three Solaris 12-meter trolley buses with Ganz electronics are in the fleet. The 3.38-km (2.1-mile) route used by the trolley buses connects a new railway station with the main part of the city. Environmental concerns prompted the establishment of this system, and wind-generated electricity is used. Landskrona, with a population of 27,000, is one of the world's smallest cities with trolley buses.

## Finland

Finland had two systems, one in Helsinki and the other in Tampere. Both systems began in the late 1940s and ended in the mid-1970s, although an experimental trolley bus operated in Helsinki for a short time in 1983. Unlike Helsinki, Tampere never had trams and relied solely on trolley buses for its main routes. Both cities operated trolley buses built by the Finnish firm Valmet.

Helsinki, Finland, installed a trolley bus system in 1940 with trolley buses built by Valmeti Oy in Finland. One of the 27 Valmet trolley buses that were in service in Helsinki is pictured. Only one route was operated and the Valmet trolley buses were the only ones to serve on the original system in Helsinki. Tampere, Finland's second-largest city, also operated trolley buses.

Tampereen Kaupungin Liikennelaitos in Tampere, Finland, had the first trolley bus system in that country. It began in 1948 and closed in 1976. A factory and manufacturing center, Tampere is a pleasant city in Finland's lake district. Three routes were in operation when this picture was taken in 1968. A fourth route had been converted to motor buses. The Valmet Model JD trolley bus pictured entered service in 1949 and served for 26 years. Valmeti Oy of Helsinki was an important manufacturer of vehicles in Finland beginning in 1945. The company built all 29 of the Tampere trolley buses. *Loring M. Lawrence*

In 1979, the Finnish firms of Sisu and Wiima built a new trolley bus for Helsinki, Finland. The trolley bus that is pictured was shown at the UITP Congress in Helsinki, and made a brief appearance under the trolley bus overhead that had not yet been removed from the streets in Helsinki. It was equipped with an auxiliary diesel engine. In 1983, plans for a new trolley bus system in Helsinki were discontinued.

## Estonia

Estonia's only trolley bus system is in the capital, Tallinn. It opened in 1965 with secondhand vehicles from Russia, and later, trolley buses from Skoda. The Tallinn trolley bus system has been a very progressive system in recent years, with well over 100 vehicles, and has recently acquired a number of new trolley buses to replace older ones.

Pictured is a close-up view of the coupling, steering, and electrical connections between a pair of Skoda 9 Tr trolley buses running in multiple. This coupling joined two of the trolley buses that operated in Tallinn, Estonia. Several cities, including Riga, Latvia, had similar coupled sets of trolley buses. This type of trolley bus operation was seen as late as the 1990s. *Loring M. Lawrence*

Tallinn, Estonia, began operating trolley buses in 1965, and the system continues today. Pictured in 1994 is this Ukrainian Yuzmash Model YuMZ articulated trolley bus that was operating on a trial basis. It was very similar to Skoda 15 Tr trolley buses, of which Tallinn had 25, but it had a larger destination sign and four doors. It was removed from service after 25,000 km in 1997. The Tallinn trolley bus service is operated by the Tallinn Tram & Trolleybus Co.

The trolley bus system in Tallinn, Estonia, had a large fleet of older trolley buses prior to the 1990s. In 1999, four two-axle Ikarus Model 412T trolley buses were added to the fleet. One is pictured here. The Tallinn trolley bus operation, the only one in Estonia, began in 1965 and continues today. The fleet numbers approximately 147 trolley buses. *Bill MacDonald*

Ten Solaris Trollino 12 low-floor trolley buses entered service in Tallinn, Estonia, in December 2002 and January 2003, updating the aging Tallinn fleet. Solaris Bus & Coach of Bolechowo, Poland, became a new producer of trolley buses in 2001. In addition to the 12-meter Trollino 12, Solaris also produces the Trollino 15, a 15-meter, 3-axle trolley bus, and the Trollino 18, an 18-meter articulated model. *Bill MacDonald*

## Latvia

Latvia was the first of the Baltic States to operate trolley buses. Its only system, in Riga, the capital, is the largest trolley bus network in the Baltics. There are more than 400 vehicles in the Riga fleet. The city is one of the last places to operate coupled-set Skoda vehicles. Many new trolley buses have been added to the Riga system recently, including buses from Russia and Poland.

In Riga, Latvia, the Riga Tramvaju un Trolejbusu Parvalde coupled together two Skoda 9 TrH trolley buses. The power poles were attached to the rear unit, but the coupled vehicles were controlled from the front vehicle. Several of these units were in service. Similar coupled units using Skoda 9 Tr trolley buses could be found in other Russian cities and also in Sofia, Bulgaria. Trolley bus service in Riga began in 1947 and continues today. It is a large system with more than 300 trolley buses.

The Tramvaju un Trolejbusu Parvalde (TTP) is one of the transit operating companies in Riga, Latvia. It and the other operating companies are under the Municipality of Riga. There is a large trolley bus system with more than 300 vehicles. Service with trolley buses in Riga began in 1947. Most of the Riga trolley buses have been Model 14 Tr Skoda vehicles. Recently, 11 BKM Model 333 articulated trolley buses built by the Belkommunmash factory in Minsk, Belarus, were acquired. One of these BKM (sometimes referred to as AAKSM) trolley buses is pictured in Riga. *Bill MacDonald*

## Lithuania

Lithuania has two trolley bus systems, in its capital, Vilnius, and in the city of Kaunas. Both cities have large urban systems and a line outside each city to recreation sites. After breaking away from communism there was difficulty getting replacement vehicles, and some used Western European trolley buses began appearing. Today more recovery has come about and new trolley buses are appearing in both cities.

Kaunas, Lithuania's second-largest city, has had a trolley bus system since 1965. With more than 200 trolley buses, the service forms the basic transportation in the city. Pictured is one of the last of nearly 100 Skoda Model 14 Tr trolley buses to operate in Kaunas. Skoda Model 15 Tr articulated trolley buses are also in the Kaunas fleet.

The Vilniaus Troleibusai in Vilnius, the capital of Lithuania, is an operating company under the Municipality of Vilnius. Trolley bus service in Vilnius began in 1956 and continues to operate today. The fleet numbers more than 300 trolley buses, most of which have been built by the Czech firm Skoda. The first Vilnius trolley buses were Skoda Model 8 Tr vehicles, followed by a large number of Model 9 Tr vehicles. Most of the present Vilnius fleet is made up of Model 14 Tr Skodas. Recently, 15 new Solaris Model 15 AC three-axle, non-articulated Trollino trolley buses have been delivered. *Bill MacDonald*

# Southern Europe
## Spain

There were 17 trolley bus systems in Spain, some being interurban services and even some operating only as freight service. Most began in the late 1940s and 1950s, and by the mid-1970s most had been discontinued. The trolley bus system in Pontevedra did not close until 1989.

The influence of trolley buses from other countries was considerable. Most cities operated vehicles manufactured elsewhere, although there were about 200 Spanish-built trolley buses.

The scene in Spain was altered dramatically with the purchase of 125 postwar double-deck trolley buses from London, beginning in 1952. Later, a few home-produced trolley buses appeared. About 25 percent of Spain's trolley bus fleet was double-deckers. Barcelona began service with Spanish-built double-deckers, but by the 1950s the single-decker was most common.

After several decades of not producing trolley buses, in recent years Spain has started manufacturing trolley buses again. The firm Hispano Carrocera has built the bodies for a large fleet of trolley buses for Quito, Ecuador, and for Merida, Venezuela.

This is one of the last trolley buses built by Maquitrans in Spain. It was delivered, with 77 others, to Tranvais de Barcelona SA between 1941 and 1953. The trolley bus system in Barcelona was the second-oldest system in Spain. It began in 1941 and ended in 1968. The trolley bus pictured was retired in 1966. *Wilhelm Pflug*

Compania del Tranvia de San Sebastian, in San Sebastian (Donostia), Spain, began operating trolley buses in 1948. The first trolley buses were built in Spain by Hispano-Suiza. One of the 25 is pictured. San Sebastian also had 25 ex-London Q-1-type double-deck buses. The service ended in 1973. There was also a small freight-only line operating trolley trucks between San Sebastian and Tolosa from 1947 to 1968. San Sebastian is in the Basque area of Spain and the name Donostia is now commonly used. *D. A. Jones London Trolley Bus Preservation Society*

Bilbao is the center of a heavily industrial area in the Basque region of northern Spain. Transportes Urbanos del Gran Bilbao operated a small trolley bus fleet between 1940 and 1978. The first trolley buses to serve in Bilbao were 10 French-built Vetra Model VCR vehicles. In 1961, 25 London Transport Q Class double-deck trolley buses were acquired. One of these is seen in downtown Bilbao in 1969. These were the last British United Traction Model 9641T trolley buses delivered to London in 1952. Bilbao trolley bus service ended in 1978. There was also a second trolley bus operation in the Bilbao area operated by the Ferrocarriles y Transportes Suburbanos de Bilbao. It was a suburban service between Bilbao and Algorta and ran from 1949 to 1963. *Loring M. Lawrence*

From 1941 into the mid-1950s four manufacturers in Spain produced trolley buses for Spanish systems. A number of other trolley buses came from France and Germany, as well as used double-deck trolley buses from London Transport. Santander in Northern Spain had two trolley bus systems. One was a small intercity line to Astillero, and the other was the city system, which began in 1951 and continued until 1970. One of the first Santander trolley buses was this one built by Hispano-Suiza in the late 1940s. La Hispano Suiza Fabrica de Automoviles SA in Barcelona dates back to 1908. Although some buses and trolley buses were built, the company was well known for trucks, cars, and engines. It later became a part of the Pegaso manufacturing group. *D. A. Jones London Trolley Bus Preservation Society*

The Compania del Tranvia de San Sebastian (Donostia), Spain, purchased 25 1952 British Electric Traction W1 trolley buses from London Transport in the early 1960s. One is pictured at the Monte Iquelplo terminus. These double-deck ex-London buses replaced Spanish-built Hispano-Suiza trolley buses, which began the San Sebastian service in 1948. They went out of service in 1972, a year prior to the closing of the trolley bus service. *Loring M. Lawrence*

Transportes Urbanos del Gran Bilbao SA, Bilbao, Spain, operated a trolley bus system between 1940 and 1978. Pictured in front of the Ayuntamiento is one of the 25, 1952 British United Traction Q1 double-deck trolley buses acquired in 1961 from England's London Transport. These trolley buses had Metropolitan-Cammell & Wagon bodywork. Bilbao was the first of 12 Spanish cities to begin trolley bus service. Note the interesting advertising for Champion spark plugs on this trolley bus. *Loring M. Lawrence*

The intercity trolley bus system in Santander, Spain, the Companie de Trolebus Santander-Astillero, began in 1955, and operated for 20 years. The first trolley buses in service were MAN Model MKE1 vehicles with Kassbohrer bodies. One is pictured here. The Santander-Astillero system also operated used double-deck trolley buses from London Transport. *D. A. Jones London Trolley Bus Preservation Society*

The City of Santander, Spain, operated trolley buses between 1951 and 1970. There were 17 trolley buses of 1955-1956 built by the Spanish firm Empresa Nacional de Autocamiones SA (Pegaso). Seven Spanish trolley bus systems operated Pegaso trolley buses. Pegaso began in 1949, following the acquisition of the Hispano-Suiza company. *D. A. Jones London Trolley Bus Preservation Society*

In the far northwestern corner of Spain is the city of La Coruna (Corunna). Its trolley bus system, Tranvia de La Coruna, began operating in 1948 and continued until 1962. Of the 51 trolley buses that served the system, 29 were acquired from London Transport in 1952. These double-deck trolley buses, one of which is pictured here, were the BUT Q1-type built in Britain around 1948. *D. A. Jones London Trolley Bus Preservation Society*

Tranvias de Zaragoza (Spain) operated trolley bus service between 1951 and 1975. This small trolley bus and four others built by the Spanish firm Pegaso were in the Zaragoza fleet. Like a number of other cities in Spain, Zaragoza operated used London Transport Q1-type trolley buses and had 12 in service. The system had three routes and a total of only 24 trolley buses. *D. A. Jones London Trolley Bus Preservation Society*

Pontevedra is a small city on the Atlantic Coast of Spain. Tranvia Electrico de Pontevedra S. operated a small trolley bus system in Pontevedra that lasted 46 years, beginning in 1943 and closing in 1989. It was the last trolley bus operation in Spain. Five trolley buses were secondhand three-axle, double-deck BUT Q1-type vehicles from London Transport. The ex-London Transport trolley bus pictured came to Pontevedra in 1964. It was built in England in the late 1940s. *D. A. Jones London Trolley Bus Preservation Society*

## Portugal

The largest trolley bus system in Portugal was in Oporto. It operated from 1959 to 1997. All the trolley buses were imported. The large fleet included the last double-deck trolley buses ever built, which came from Lancia in Italy.

There were two other trolley bus systems in Portugal. The city of Braga began its system with trolley buses imported from a trolley bus system in Germany. Coimbra's system was the first in Portugal and continues today.

Coimbra is Portugal's fifth largest city and home of a distinguished university founded in 1290. The first trolley bus route opened in 1947 serving a hilly neighborhood across the River Mondego. Portugal had two other trolley bus systems, but the service operated by Servicos Municipalizados de Transportes Coimbra is the only trolley bus system remaining today. Pictured is one of six Sunbeam Model MF 2NS trolley buses that entered service in 1966. Built in England, they had UTIC/British Thompson-Houston bodywork. Livery is yellow and cream. *Loring M. Lawrence*

Servicos Municipalizados de Braga (Portugal) began a trolley bus system in 1963, replacing a tram service. The system began with the purchase of the entire fleet of nine vehicles from the trolley bus system in Heilbron, Germany. Pictured is one of the three ex-Heilbron MAN trolley buses with Kassbohrer bodywork and Siemens electrical equipment. Henschel in Germany built the six other trolley buses in the fleet. The trolley bus system in the small city of Braga closed in 1979. *Collection of Cliff Scholes*

Sociedade de Transportes Collectivos de Porto SA, in Oporto, Portugal, began operating trolley buses in 1959. In 1968 a fleet of 50 double-deck trolley buses became the backbone of the Oporto trolley bus fleet. Dalfa in Portugal built the bodies on Italian Lancia chassis. These trolley buses were the last double-deck trolley buses built in the world. They ended service in 1995, and the Oporto trolley bus system closed its doors two years later.

Pictured here is the last of 24 single-deck trolley buses delivered to the Sociedade de Transportes Collectivos de Porto SA, Oporto, Portugal, in 1968. Lancia in Italy built these trolley buses, similar to the 50 double-deck units delivered at the same time. The double-deck trolley buses went out of service in 1995, but the single-deck trolley buses continued until 1997.

Trolley bus service began in Coimbra, Portugal, in 1947, and Coimbra is currently the only Portuguese city that continues to operate trolley buses. Saurer in Switzerland built the first Coimbra trolley buses. Today, there is a fleet of 20 trolley buses built by the Portuguese firm Salvador Caetano of Vila Nova de Gaia near Oporto. The Servicos Municipalizados de Transportes de Coimbra is the name of the operator.

## Italy

Italy has a long history of trolley bus operations dating back to the early 1900s. More than a dozen cities have retained trolley bus systems. New systems opened in Genova in 1997 and in Rome in 2005, a sign of changes in legislation favorable to trolley bus systems. Previously, Rome had a large fleet of trolley buses, which operated between 1937 and 1972. Milano was one of the first large, permanent systems in Italy, as well as in Europe, and continues to operate today, although considerably downsized. Naples has two systems and has recently replaced its vehicles with modern equipment.

Manufacture of trolley buses has been important in Italy. In addition to supplying their own country with vehicles, after World War II Italian manufacturers built up a good market in Europe and elsewhere in the world, particularly in South America, exporting trolley buses to countries that did not produce their own. Several Italian manufacturers responded to the new market, using different bodywork suppliers. Early trolley buses in Italy had the unique central or right-hand driving positions, but today follow the normal left-hand driving position.

An interesting modern experiment, which so far does not appear to have been successful, occurred with a trolley bus that was introduced in Trieste. It did not involve overhead wires, which is an objection to trolley buses in many cities, but had a conduit in the middle of the street. The power to the vehicle came from the lower part of this conduit, and a tether connected the trolley bus to the conduit. The trolley bus could be maneuvered to either side of the conduit.

Fiat and Alfa Romeo were the leading Italian trol-

This Fiat Model 668F/131 with a Viberti body was one of 10 trolley buses delivered to the Aziende Municipalizzate di Modena in Modena, Italy, in 1950. They were part of the original fleet of trolley buses that began the service in 1950. Trolley buses continue to operate in Modena today. Ten MAN trolley buses with Autodromo bodies are the newest in the Modena fleet.

ley bus builders for many years and exported many vehicles. Another Italian firm, Lancia, built many trolley buses for the home market and also for export. Compagnia Generale di Electricita (CGE) and Tecnomasio Italiano Brown Boveri, SpA (TIBB) have been important Italian suppliers of trolley bus motors and electrics. Another Italian company, AnsaldoBreda, currently produces trolley buses and is an important supplier of motors and electrics. Autodromo is also building modern trolley buses.

The private Italian company Autoindustriale Torino began a small interurban trolley bus service in 1950. It operated over Selle di Pino pass on a steep and winding 12-km route between Torino and Chiere. Pictured is one of the 11 Fiat 668F trolley buses with Viberti bodies that operated on the service. They were built in 1951/52, and continued to operate until 1979, when Azienda Tranvie Municipali (now known as Azienda Torinese Mobilita) acquired the system and replaced the trolley buses with motor buses. The route was one of the few intercity trolley bus services. *Wilhelm Pflug*

Azienda Tranviaria Municipale - Milano (Italy) acquired 10 of these Breda-bodied Alfa Romeo Model 140 AF trolley buses in 1951. Trolley bus service in Milano began in 1933 and continues today. The system, now known as Azienda Trasporti Municipali di Milano, has been downsized from the almost 400 trolley buses that Milano had at its peak. Alfa Romeo of Torino, Italy, not only built many trolley buses for Italy but also exported many vehicles.

The Azienda Tranvie Municipali Torino (ATM) (now Azienda Torinese Mobilita) in Torino, Italy, took delivery of this Fiat Model 2401 FM trolley bus and 11 others in 1953. The ATM began running trolley buses in 1931 and the service continued to 1980. There were 43 trolley buses when the service was discontinued. Interestingly, this trolley bus on Route 54 indicated it operated from the Torino suburb of Lingotto. Lingotto was the home of the Fiat factory where this trolley bus may have been built.

Azienda Tranviaria Municipale in Milano, Italy, added 25 of these Fiat Model 672F vehicles with Cansa bodies in 1951. The driving position on the right side was very common for trolley buses in Italy at the time. Many Italian trolley buses of the period also had large balloon tires and three axles. Fiat built its first trolley buses in 1931 and was a major trolley bus producer in Italy, mainly for the home market.

Trolley bus service in Alessandria, Italy, began in 1952 and was operated by the Azienda Riunita Filovia a Autolinee SpA. The first vehicles were eight Fiat Model 666F trolley buses with Casara bodies, one of which is pictured here. Trolley bus service ended in Alessandria in 1974.

La Societe Transports Elettrici Liguri (STEL), in San Remo, Italy, began operating a picturesque interurban trolley bus line in 1955. Ventimiglia is on the west end of the line and Taggia at the east end. It passes through San Remo, the main city in the area. In 1957, 21 Fiat Model 2411 trolley buses with Cansa bodies were introduced. The Model 2411 was built between 1955 and 1965. Fiat also built other trolley bus models, producing about 430 during that period. The STEL system is now known as the Riviera Transporti. It is located in Imperia and continues to operate the interurban route.

Five Fiat Model 2401 trolley buses, one of which is pictured here, went into service in Ancona, Italy, in 1957 for the Azienda Trasporti Municipalizzata Autofiloviari (ATMA). Trolley bus service began in Ancona in 1949. The trolley bus service in Ancona continues and is now operated by Conerobus. Ancona also had a suburban trolley bus system, Filovia Provincial Ancona Falconara, which began in 1948 and ended in 1972.

Torino, Italy, was one of the first large cities in Italy to establish trolley bus service. The system was known as the Azienda Tranvie Municipali Torino. It began operating trolley buses in 1931 with three Fiat Model 461F vehicles. The last trolley buses to operate ATM services in Torino were 15 Viberti-bodied Fiat Model 2405 articulated units, one of which is pictured here in 1958. Torino trolley bus services ended in 1980 after nearly 50 years. Interestingly, Torino had three other trolley bus operators, mainly serving suburban areas.

Naples, Italy, has two trolley bus systems. The largest is Azienda Napoletana Mobilita. It began under the name Azienda Tranvie e Autofilovie del Commune di Napoli. Seventy-eight Alfa Romeo trolley buses joined the fleet in 1961-1962. One is pictured here in Piazza Garibaldi in the center of Naples. These trolley buses served for 40 years. Recently, 68 new trolley buses were added.

Rimini, a popular resort city on Italy's Adriatic Sea, has operated a one-route trolley bus system since 1939, and continues to do so today. Pictured is one of the 17 Volvo B59 trolley buses with Mauri bodies that were delivered in 1979. The route is 14 km, mainly along the coast to Riccione. Roadwork has caused suspension of trolley bus service several times in recent years.

Departing from the railway station in Ancona, Italy, is this 1983 Fiat Model F201 trolley bus of the Azienda Trasporti Municipalizzata Autofiloviari. It was one of nine trolley buses with bodies by Menarini operating the five-route trolley bus service in Ancona.

The Aziende Industrial Municipalizzate, Vicenza, Italy, began trolley bus service in 1928 with two routes and 16 trolley buses. The service ended in 1970. Pictured is one of five trolley buses that entered service in Vicenza in 1953. They had Savigliano chassis and electric equipment and Garavini bodies.

Riviera Transporti in San Remo, Italy, has a modern trolley bus system. It consists mainly of a long route along the Ligurian Sea between Ventimiglia, near the Principality of Monaco, and Taggia to the east. Pictured in 1996 is one of 14 Breda Model 4001 trolley buses added to the system in 1991. Trolley buses first began operating in the San Remo area in 1942.

A variety of trolley buses have been in service by the Azienda Trasporti Municipali di Milano (ATM) in Milano, Italy, since trolley bus service began in 1933. In 1992, 33 Bredabus Model 4001 IB trolley buses were acquired. One is seen operating the circular Route 91, which is one of the trolley bus routes that continue to operate today. In 1975 there were 10 ATM trolley bus routes, and earlier the system had as many as 19 routes.

La Spezia on Italy's Ligurian Sea began trolley bus service in 1951. It continues today and is now operated by Consorzio Transporte La Spezia. Pictured in 1995 is an Italian Breda Model 4001 122 trolley bus, one of 14 acquired by the system in 1988. The three routes operated in La Spezia require only 14 trolley buses. An earlier two-vehicle trolley bus service operated between 1906 and 1909.

The Azienda Energetica Municipalizzata has operated a small trolley bus system in Cremona, Italy, since 1940. It continues to operate, although recently there has been some concern that trolley bus services would be discontinued. In 1999, two new Breda trolley buses, one of which is pictured here, were acquired for the Cremona service. Electrical equipment on these vehicles is by Ansaldo.

Although this articulated Neoplan vehicle could be considered a trolley bus, it had some distinct differences. An experiment by the Italian firm AnsaldoBreda in 2000, it was considered for service in Trieste, Italy, by the Azienda Consorziale Trasporti (ACT), but did not materialize. The vehicle received its electrical power from a street conduit. There was a type of tether arrangement between the conduit and the vehicle to allow it to maneuver to various positions on the street. Trieste had a fairly sizable normal trolley bus system in the past, beginning in 1935 and discontinuing in 1975.

Trolley bus service returned to Rome, Italy, in 2005 with 30 Solaris Trollino 18 duobuses. The new trolley buses operate using overhead wires over part of the route, but switch to battery power when operating in the central part of the city. This is to avoid having overhead wires, which are considered objectionable, in the central area. The recent introduction of trolley buses is the second trolley bus operation in Rome. Between 1937 and 1973 there was an extensive trolley bus operation in the city. It was one of the largest systems in Europe with more than 400 trolley buses. *Solaris*

Beginning in mid-2000, the first of 109 new AnsaldoBreda Model F19 trolley buses were entering service for the Azienda Napoletana Mobilita (ANM) in Naples, Italy. Pictured is the second of the new trolley buses acquired. The AnsaldoBreda trolley buses are modern low-floor vehicles. The ANM is one of two trolley bus systems in Naples. It is the larger system and began in 1940. The other trolley bus system is the Compagnia Trasporte Pubblici (CTP), which began in 1964. Both continue to operate. The Ansaldo Trasporte, an electrical equipment manufacturer, and Breda Menarinibus SPA, a bus manufacturer, merged in 1999.

Bologna, Italy, has had three trolley bus systems. The first one began in 1940 and closed in 1945. Another system began 10 years later and closed in 1982. In 1991 the present system began. The operator is Azienda Trasporti Consorziali Bologna (ATC). In October 2002 an order was placed for 49 Irisbus Cristalis 18.5-meter trolley buses. The first of these new trolley buses was delivered in 2005 and is pictured. These trolley buses have the Siemens Transportation Systems guiding system. *Nicolas Tellier*

## Greece

Greece has had two trolley bus systems, one in Athens and one in Pireaus. Although the Greek systems began operations fairly late, the country has a distinction in that no significant part of either of its systems has been discontinued. Pireaus began service in 1948 using 12 Fiat trolley buses that continued in service until 1983. The two systems share common management, and are joined by wires, but there is no through service.

Between 1953 and 1960, the British-owned company that ran the trolley bus system in Athens at that time ordered a fleet of 126 Alfa Romeo and Lancia trolley buses from Italy. The system experienced modest growth in the 1970s using secondhand trolley buses from Italy. A major expansion took place in the late 1970s, when the harmful effects of motor vehicle exhausts were recognized. The city is quite hilly and pollution is a concern. The system had 360 Soviet-built trolley buses including one of the early ZIU-683 prototype articulated trolley buses. New vehicles were built by Van Hool and Neoplan and replaced many of the trolley buses in Athens prior to the city's hosting of the 2004 Olympics.

Fiat, the Italian builder of trolley buses, was one of the largest trolley bus producers in Western Europe. In 1940 Fiat built eleven 9-meter Model 656 trolley buses to operate in Pireaus, Greece. However, because of World War II the trolley buses were not delivered until 1949, when they operated on short routes in the harbor area of Pireaus. Athens-Pireaus Area Electric Buses (ILPAP) is the name of the system now operating trolley buses in the Athens-Pireaus area.

Around 1963, 47 Italian-built Lancia trolley buses entered service in Athens, Greece. These joined Italian Alfa Romeo trolley buses in the large Athens system. The hilly terrain in Athens was well suited to trolley bus operations. In 1963 the fleet numbered 136 trolley buses. That total grew to 216 by 1982, and 403 in 1994. The Athens area had two trolley bus systems, a large one in Athens and a small one in the port city of Pireaus. They are now merged.

Pictured is one of the 96 Van Hool Model A300T trolley buses acquired for Athens-Pireaus Area Electric Buses (ILPAP), Athens, Greece. Delivery of these new trolley buses was a part of the renewal of older vehicles that began in 1999 and continued to 2001. Athens wanted to update its trolley bus fleet prior to the city's hosting of the 2004 Summer Olympic Games. Trolley buses were first introduced in Athens in 1953. *Wilhelm Pflug*

The German firm Neoplan began delivering 112 new Model N601 4E trolley buses to Athens-Pireaus Area Electric Buses (ILPAP) in Athens, Greece, in 1999. One of the new trolley buses for fleet renewal prior to the 2004 Olympic Games is pictured here. Prior to that time, Athens had Uritsky ZIU, Alfa Romeo, and Lancia trolley buses in service, and they were, in some cases, beyond their useful life. *Wilhelm Pflug*

## Serbia

Serbia, a part of the former Yugoslavia, established a trolley bus system in Beograd in 1946. It is a very large system and continues to operate in the capital today. Early vehicles were Italian built. Later, home-produced vehicles were added under license from Italian companies. Many of the recent trolley buses in Beograd have come from Russia, including some very new ones from the Trolza Company, formerly the Uritsky Company.

## Bosnia

The civil war in Bosnia in 1992 marked the end of the only trolley bus system in that country at the time. It was started in Sarajevo in 1984, the year the Winter Olympics were held there, and included a five-route system. Much of the infrastructure was destroyed during the war. Operations have resumed, with new and secondhand vehicles from the Czech Republic, Germany, and the Netherlands.

Belgrade, Serbia (Yugoslavia), has operated a large trolley bus system since 1947. The present operator, Gradski Saobracaj Preduzece Beograde, currently has 135 trolley buses, most of which were built by the Uritsky Company in Russia. Pictured is a Uritsky ZIU trolley bus, one of 51 acquired in the 1970s. The original trolley buses in Belgrade were 30 Fiat Model 668F vehicles. *O. Iskov*

This Trolza Model 62052 is one of 10 that went into service for the Gradski Saobracaj Preduzece Beograde in Belgrade, Serbia (Yugoslavia), in 2002. The Trolza company, Trollejbusny Zavod, is the new name of the Uritsky Company in Russia. Belgrade was one of the first cities to receive the Model 6252. It had a newly designed front including a large destination sign. *O. Iskov*

# Eastern Europe
## *Hungary*

Budapest has a very large trolley bus system. The present system opened in 1949. The Budapest transport system has been very efficient in refurbishing its vehicles, and some of the refurbished trolley buses operating in Budapest are in almost new condition. There are two other systems in Hungary, in Debrecen and Szeged.

The Hungarian firm Ikarus has been one of the world's largest producers of buses and trolley buses. Its trolley buses have been exported to many countries, especially in Eastern Europe. The company has developed new trolley bus designs since the 1990s, and a number of new Ikarus trolley buses are operating in Budapest. Some others have been sold to fleets in other countries.

The Debreceni Kozlekedesi Vallalat (DKV) in the city of Debrecen in the Puszta region of Hungary didn't begin operating trolley buses on its streets until 1985. The service continues today. Russian-built Uritsky ZIU trolley buses were first used, and the ZIU pictured was acquired in 1988. It was refurbished in 2003. A total of 34 ZIU trolley buses have been operated in Debrecen, along with some Ikarus articulated trolley buses. The DKV has been evaluating several new models of trolley buses, and 21 Solaris Model 12T trolley buses are being delivered.

Trolley bus service began in Szeged, Hungary, with 10 Russian ZIU trolley buses. The system grew, and in the early 1990s ten Skoda Model 15 Tr articulated trolley buses were acquired. Five routes are operated and more than 50 trolley buses are required. The Szegedi Kozlekedesi Vallalat operates the system.

Pictured is one of the 15 Ikarus/Kiepe low-floor Model IK 412T trolley buses that were put into service in 2002 in Budapest, Hungary. The present Budapest trolley bus service is operated by the Budapesti Kozlekedesi Vallalat (BKV). It began in 1949, and has been a large trolley bus system over the years. Currently there are more than 100 trolley buses in its fleet.

The Budapesti Kozlekedesi Vallalat (BKV), Budapest, Hungary, began operating trolley buses in 1949, and the service continues. However, there was a small system that operated in Budapest from 1933 to 1944. Since the 1970s ZIU Model 682 trolley buses have operated much of the BKV trolley bus network. This ZIU trolley bus, pictured in 2004, entered service in the early 1980s and has since been refurbished. More than 200 ZIU trolley buses have operated in Budapest in addition to older Ikarus Model 280 trolley buses.

Prague, Czech Republic, had one of the early trolley bus systems. It began in 1936 and closed in 1972. However, there have been some indications that trolley buses may return to Prague. Three Czech trolley bus manufacturers, Praga, Tatra, and Skoda, built trolley buses for Prague. Pictured is one of the 135 Model T 400 Tatra trolley buses that served Prague from 1955. In 1961 the trolley bus fleet reached its maximum of 178 vehicles.

## Czech Republic

Except for one early operation, trolley bus systems in the Czech Republic began late, but the country now has one of the most thriving trolley bus operations in the world. There have been 18 modern trolley bus systems there, and only three have been discontinued. The rest continue to operate. Trolley buses have popular support as environmentally friendly transportation, especially in the towns of the northwest where heavy industry contributes to pollution.

Trolley buses experienced strong growth between 1940 and 1952, but access to automobiles has reduced passenger numbers. New systems have opened, including one of the largest in Usti nad Labem. The latest system to be established was in 1995 in Chomutov.

The trolley bus system in Brno began in 1949 with Skoda vehicles operating on three lines. In the late 1960s it looked like the service would close. It continued, however, with trolley buses serving new housing developments in the suburbs. A new route opened in 1971, with others following. A total of 141 vehicles operate on a 54.3-km overhead network.

Prague had the only large early system, with three-axle vehicles of several types driving on the left. They are reported to be the only trolley buses anywhere in the world to be rebuilt from left- to right-hand drive as a result of a change in the rule of the road. The Prague system closed in 1972.

Skoda, the Czech Republic trolley bus manufacturer, has been a large builder of trolley buses for many years. Since 1936 Skoda has built more than 12,000 trolley buses, the greatest number of trolley buses built by any one manufacturer outside Russia. Skoda continues today, but has a partnership with Irisbus that supplies bodies through its subsidiary company Karosa. Skoda has exported trolley buses to systems in the United States as well as many other countries.

Brno, Czech Republic, has had a large trolley bus fleet since 1949. Pictured is this early Skoda Model 9 Tr trolley bus. It went into service in Brno in 1979 along with 46 others. Dopravni podnik mesta Brna, as, operator of the transit system in Brno, no longer operates Model 9 Tr trolley buses, but recently added 43 new Skoda 21 Tr and four Skoda 22 Tr trolley buses.

This Skoda Model 14 Tr trolley bus went into service in Hradec Kralove, Czech Republic, in 1989. The service of Dopravni podnik mesta Hradec Kralove sp began in 1949 and continues today with seven trolley bus routes and 35 Skoda trolley buses.

At the end of the 20th Century the city of Usti nad Labem, Czech Republic, celebrated its 75th anniversary. It was also the 100th anniversary of public transport in the city. Trolley buses have operated since 1965. There are 10 routes, some of which are quite hilly. This Skoda Model 15 Tr BH6 trolley bus and four others were delivered in 1995, when this picture was taken.

One of the more than 60 Skoda 14 Tr standard trolley buses delivered to the Plzenske mestske dopravni podniky in Pilsen, Czech Republic, was pictured in 1995. At that time, this trolley bus was advertising the 700th anniversary of Pilsen. The Pilsen system was one of the first trolley bus systems in the Czech Republic, beginning in 1941.

The city of Ceske Budejovice in the Czech Republic has the distinction of having three trolley bus systems in the 20th Century. The first began in 1909 with two vehicles and ended in 1914. The second began in 1948 and closed in 1971. The latest system, which continues, opened in 1991. The trolley bus pictured, a Skoda Model 14 Tr 07-10.7, was in the group of trolley buses which helped get the latest system established. *O. Iskov*

A Skoda 14 Tr 0510 of the Dopravni podnik Ostrava, as, is seen passing the Church of the Divine Saviour in downtown Ostrava, Czech Republic. Ostrava began trolley bus service in 1952, and it continues with a fleet of approximately 45 trolley buses. The system, which also has trams and buses, serves a wide area that includes many suburban villages.

Marianske Lanze is a spa city in the Bohemia area of the Czech Republic. It has a trolley bus service operated by Dopravni podnik Marianske Lanze, with three routes. Five Skoda 14 Tr vehicles are in service, one of which is pictured here in 1995. With a population of 15,000, Marianske Lanze is the smallest city of the 13 Czech Republic cities with trolley buses. The first trolley bus service began in the city in 1952 using Skoda 7 Tr models. The city has been a consistent user of Skoda trolley buses.

The Dopravni podnik mesta Chomutova Jirkova of Chomutov, Czech Republic, has only been in operation since 1995. It is the newest of 13 trolley bus systems operating in that country. Four interurban routes are operated with the original fleet of 25 Skoda 15 Tr articulated trolley buses. One of the fleet is pictured here, three months after the service began.

Dopravni podnik mesta Pardubice, as, is the company which operates the 13 trolley bus routes in Pardubice, Czech Republic. Trolley bus service in Pardubice began in 1952 with nine Skoda Model 7 Tr 1 vehicles. Pictured is one of the newer Skoda Model 14 Tr 17.6M trolley buses, delivered in 1996 with three similar trolley buses. The system continues today.

The two Skoda Model 21 Tr trolley buses pictured are operated by the Dopravni podnik mesta Brna, in Brno, Czech Republic. The Brno trolley bus system, which began in 1949, is the largest in the Czech Republic. In 1999, soon after the Skoda Model 21 Tr was introduced, Brno acquired 44 of the new Skoda trolley buses. The year commemorated 50 years of trolley buses in the city.

The company Dopravni Spolecnost Zlin-Otrokovice, sro (DSZO) began trolley bus service in Zlin and Otrokovice in the Czech Republic in 1944 and continues to operate with approximately 60 vehicles. A 12-km (7.5-mi.) interurban route connects Zlin and Otrokovice. Pictured in Otrokovice, where the area's major railway station is located, is a Skoda 15 Tr 13 6M trolley bus delivered in 1999. Zlin, which was called Gottwaldov during the communist years, has been recognized worldwide for shoe manufacturing.

The prototype Model 24 Tr low-floor trolley bus built by the partnership of Skoda, Irisbus, and Karosa was acquired in early 2005 by the Dopravini podnik Marianske Lanze (Czech Republic). It is seen in the prototype colors as it passes one of the spas in Marianske Lanze. There had been some concern that trolley buses would be discontinued in Marianske Lanze, but the acquisition of this new trolley bus may indicate that trolley bus service will continue. *Petr Kasencak, Skoda Electric*

In 2003 Solaris introduced the first 15-meter rigid trolley bus. It was built in a partnership with the Ostrava, Czech Republic, trolley bus system. Pictured is the prototype Trollino 15 AC Solaris operating in Ostrava. Motor buses of 15 meters have been very popular in many European countries for a number of years.

Dopravni Spolecnost Zlin-Otrokovice is the trolley bus operator in Zlin and Otrokovice, Czech Republic. It also operates an interurban route between the two cities. The system was the first to place an order for the new Skoda/Irisbus/Karosa 24 Tr trolley buses. The first low-floor model in the five-vehicle order is pictured here. Skoda Electric sro operated a trolley bus factory known as Skoda Ostrov in Ostrov, Czech Republic, which was closed in 2004. The new partnership builds the Model 24 Tr trolley bus using Skoda Electric electronics and Irisbus bodies. The bodies are sent ckd from France to the Czech Republic for completion in the Karosa factory in Vysoke Myto. *Petr Kasencak, Skoda Electric*

## Slovakia

Bratislava, the capital, had an early trolley bus system beginning in 1909. It operated with only seven vehicles and lasted just five or six years. In 1941 a new system was established, which continues today, with more than 100 vehicles in service. Most vehicles are Skodas, but the system still had Skoda-Sanos articulated vehicles until 1998. Slovakia has opened three new systems since 1989, making a total of five systems currently operating. There are trolley bus systems in all the major cities in Slovakia.

Bratislava, the capital and largest city in Slovakia, operated a small trolley bus system for 10 years beginning in 1905. In 1941 trolley buses were reintroduced in Bratislava. Pictured in 1994 was this Skoda 14 Tr 008 5 trolley bus that went into service in the late 1980s. Bratislava had Skoda-Sanos articulated trolley buses in the 1980s, prior to 1988 when Skoda began building 15 Tr articulated trolley buses. The system in Bratislava is operated by Dopravny podnik hl. mesta Bratislavy as. The first Bratislava trolley buses were 14 MAN Siemans vehicles.

Banska Bystrica is a picturesque city in a mountainous area of Slovakia. Trolley bus service was established by the Dopravny podnik mesta Banska Bystrica with eight Skoda 14 Tr standard trolley buses. Soon after the service began, 28 articulated Skoda 15 Tr trolley buses, one of which is pictured here, went into service. The trolley bus service in Banska Bystrica is now closed.

The Dopravny podnik mesta Kosic, Sp of Kosice, Slovakia, has one of the newer trolley bus systems in Slovakia. It started in 1993. The service began with 15 Skoda Model 15 Tr 10.7 articulated trolley buses, one of which is pictured here in 2002. Two trolley bus routes are in operation and further expansion is expected in the future.

Zilina is the newest of the five trolley bus systems in Slovakia. Service was established in 1994 by the Dopravni podnik mesta Ziliny. Pictured is a Skoda Model 14 Tr 14 7 passing by the railway station. The system started with one route but additional routes using Skoda articulated Model 15 Tr 10 7 trolley buses are being started. The first Model 14 Tr Skoda trolley buses are now in service. The first Model 14 Tr Skoda buses began service in 1981.

## Poland

Only the cities of Lublin and Gdynia have extensive trolley bus systems today. However, the city of Tychy began a small system in 1982. The city of Poznan began operating trolley buses in 1930 and continued for some 40 years. A system began in Warsaw in 1946. It was a very large system that ceased operations in 1973. Ten years later trolley buses reappeared in Warsaw, but trolley bus service finally ended in Warsaw in 1995.

A large variety of imported vehicles have been used in Poland over the years, but the development of Jelcz trolley buses in the late 1990s, which were patterned after the trolley buses built by Renault in France, contributed to the survival of several systems. With the opening of the Solaris factory, Poland has become a very important builder of trolley buses in the 21st Century. Trolley buses built by Solaris have been appearing in cities throughout Europe.

One of the 12 cities in Poland that operated trolley buses was Slupsk, near the Baltic Sea in Northwestern Poland. The service began in 1985 and ended in 1999. One of the original 10 ZIU-9 Russian-built trolley buses for Slupsk is pictured. The Slupsk service also operated 16 Polish-built Jelcz Model PR 110E trolley buses. *Bohdan Turzanski*

Debica, Poland, operated 10 trolley buses on two routes for only two years, from 1988 to 1990. Pictured is one of the Polish-built Jelcz Model PR 110E trolley buses that entered service in 1988. Debica is a city divided by a railroad. The south side has the city center and most of the housing. The north side had the Igloopol agricultural-industrial plant and some housing. The trolley buses only operated on the north side, and didn't serve the city center. This was because of a lack of bridges over the railways and political disagreements between the city and officials of Igloopol. *Bohdan Turzanski*

Pictured is one of the four Fiat Model 418AC motor buses originally in service in Vicenza, Italy, which was converted to a trolley bus in 1994 for service in Lublin, Poland. One of these trolley buses is pictured on a route operated by the Miejski Przedseinbiorstwo Komunikaiji in Lublin.

Lublin, Poland, has had a large fleet of trolley buses since service began in 1953. From 1972 to 1977, 136 Russian-built Uritsky ZIU trolley buses were acquired. One of the first is pictured here. Most of the ZIU trolley buses have been replaced. In 1994, four Fiat trolley buses that were formerly motor buses operating in Vicenza, Italy, went into service in Lublin, joining a large number of Polish-built Jelcz trolley buses. Electrical equipment from these vehicles was fitted to some Jelcz models. *O. Iskov*

Warsaw, Poland, has had two trolley bus systems in the 20th Century. The first began in 1946 with six routes, and ended in 1973. Ten years later a new trolley bus service was inaugurated in Warsaw. It was a one-route system in the south part of the city that entered the suburb of Plaseczno. On advice of consultants it was discontinued in 1995. Pictured are two Polish-built Jelcz trolley buses that were acquired new: the one in front in 1991 and the one behind in 1990. Several 1957-1958 trolley buses with trailers from the St. Gallen, Switzerland, system were added to the Warsaw fleet in 1992. Miejskie Zaklady Autobusowe operated the service.

Pictured in 1999 is a 1988 Jelcz PR110 Kapena trolley bus operated by the Miejski Przedseinbiorstwo Komunikaiji in Lublin, Poland. It was one of 82 trolley buses in service in Lublin at that time. Lublin began operating trolley buses in 1953 and the service has continued. This system and the system in Gdynia have been the largest in Poland, both having some 80 trolley buses.

After World War I Poland did not have its own port on the Baltic Sea. As a result, the city of Gdynia was transformed from a small village to a large city, and an important Polish seaport. By 1943 a sizable trolley bus system was established, which continues today. The Jelcz company began building trolley buses in the 1970s and has supplied Gdynia with many since that time. Pictured is one of the two Jelcz trolley buses delivered to Gdynia in 1991. The first Jelcz trolley bus in Gdynia was acquired in 1977.

Tychy is a small city in Poland near Katowice. Tychy began a four-route trolley bus system in 1992 that continues today. Pictured is one of the two new Solaris trolley buses that were delivered in 2003. It was painted blue and white and featured full advertising, which is different from the usual all-yellow color for other Tychy trolley buses. The service is operated by Tychy-Tyskie Linie Trolejbusowe Spolka z. o. o.

## Romania

For a number of years Romania has been quite favorable to trolley bus systems. Nineteen systems continue to operate, with many of the small cities having trolley bus fleets of as few as 10 vehicles. Several of these small-city systems have been established in the last 10 or 12 years.

The largest system, in Bucharest, was established in 1950. Actually, Bucharest has two separate systems that are not joined, even though the same operator, Regia Autonoma de Transport Bucuresti (RATB), runs them. The system in the southeast section of the city has several routes. It operates vehicles that originally came from Switzerland as motor buses and have been converted to trolley buses.

Trolley bus manufacturing has been quite important in Romania. Romanian manufacturers have produced most of the trolley buses in use there; although some used trolley buses have come from Western European countries, including Switzerland, Germany, and France. New trolley buses are appearing in Romania today. Some have come from Hungary and the Czech Republic, but the Romanian manufacturer ROCAR has built most of the trolley buses operating in Romanian cities.

Sibiu, Romania, has only operated trolley buses for approximately 23 years. Except for 12 articulated and standard trolley buses built by the Romanian ROCAR firm, other vehicles have been FBW trolley buses from Switzerland. Pictured is a 1966 FBW trolley bus that was originally in service in Biel, Switzerland. *O. Iskov*

Timisoara had one of the first trolley bus systems in Romania, beginning in 1940, and it continues to operate, after 65 years, with about 81 vehicles. Today's Timisoara system is operated by the Regia Autonoma de Transport Timisoara (RATT). Many of the Timisoara trolley buses are secondhand, coming from France, Germany, and Austria. The trolley bus pictured is a 1978 Berliet Model ER100R that was originally in the Lyon, France, fleet. More than half of the RATT fleet consists of Berliet and Renault trolley buses from Lyon.

Three Daimler-Benz 0305 trolley buses, which originally operated in Esslingen, Germany, went to Timisoara, Romania, for service by the Regia Autonoma de Transport Timisoara (RATT) in 2000. Timisoara had its first trolley bus service in 1941.

Brasov, Romania, has a large trolley bus operation administered by the Regia Autonoma de Transport Brasov (RATB). Most of the Brasov trolley buses have been built by ROCAR in Romania. However, Brasov has acquired a few trolley buses from elsewhere. Pictured is a 1983 Mercedes-Benz trolley bus originally operated by the Basler Verkehrs-Betriebe, Basel, Switzerland, and acquired by the RATB in 2000. It is possible that Brasov trolley bus service will be discontinued.

Bucharest is the capital and largest city in Romania. Its transit system is known as the Regia Autonoma de Transport Bucuresti (RATB). It has a large trolley bus operation, including a three-route service in the southeast section of the city that is not connected with the center of the city and the large concentration of RATB trolley bus routes. The pictured Saurer trolley bus is unusual. It came from the transit system in Zurich, Switzerland, where it operated as a diesel bus. It was converted to a trolley bus in Bucharest.

ROCAR, a Romanian manufacturer, has built all 57 of the articulated trolley buses operated by the Regia Autonoma de Transport Bucuresti (RATB) in Bucharest, Romania. All were added since 1989; one is pictured here. Some two-axle ROCAR trolley buses are also in RATB service.

The Regia Autonoma de Transport Bucuresti (RATB) in Bucharest, Romania, has a large trolley bus system, with 274 vehicles in service. Since 1997, RATB has been renewing its fleet with Ikarus/Astra trolley buses. Through 2002, 180 two-axle units have entered service. These trolley buses were built by the partnership of Ikarus in Hungary and the Romanian builder Astra Bus. Bucharest began trolley bus service in 1950.

Sibiu, Romania, has a picturesque city center thanks to its architectural heritage. Trolley bus service in Sibiu began in 1983 and continues today. SC "Tursib" SA operates it. A number of the Sibiu trolley buses are second-hand FBW vehicles from Lausanne and Biel in Switzerland. However, there are 11 Romanian-built ROCAR Model 212E trolley buses in service, eight being two-axle models as in this 1997 picture. There are also some articulated trolley buses in service. *Loring M. Lawrence*

Regia Autonoma de Transport Cluj-Napoca is the trolley bus operation in Cluj-Napoca, Romania. It has the second-oldest trolley bus operation in Romania, which began in 1948. The fleet operates approximately 100 trolley buses. Pictured is a 1992 ROCAR articulated, one of 70 similar articulated trolley buses that were first acquired in 1986. *O. Iskov*

Pictured is the prototype trolley bus built by the partnership of Astra Bus in Arad, Romania, and Irisbus of France. The bodies for these trolley buses are built by Irisbus in France and sent in ckd form to the Astra Bus factory in Arad where they are completed and electronics are installed. Regia Autonoma de Transport Cluj-Napoca (Romania) received the first five of these new trolley buses in 2004.

## Bulgaria

Sofia, the capital of Bulgaria, and its largest city, operated its first trolley bus system from 1941 to 1944. The system in service in Sofia today began in 1948 and has a large fleet in operation. Since 1985 there have been more than a dozen new systems and system expansions, and 15 cities now operate trolley bus systems in Bulgaria. Bulgarian-built trolley buses manufactured by Chavdar in Botevgrad have appeared in some cities. A number of secondhand vehicles have been acquired, but newer trolley buses are being delivered from other manufacturers.

## Moldova

Moldova shares much with its western neighbor, Romania, but unlike Romania did not develop trolley bus systems until after its absorption within the Soviet Union. It has a large system in the capital, Chisinau, with more than 400 trolley buses. That system started in 1949.

The Sofia (Bulgaria) Public Transport Company Elektrotransport AD operates the Sofia trolley bus system. The first trolley buses operated in Sofia in 1941, and the one-route, three-vehicle system lasted only three years. Then, in 1948, a new trolley bus system was established and continues today with more than 150 trolley buses. The majority of the fleet are Ikarus Model 280T92 articulated trolley buses that were acquired between 1985 and 1988. The 1988 Ikarus 280T92 trolley bus pictured is on the busy Silvintsa Boulevard in Sofia's center.

This Tramcar Model TK/130 is a prototype trolley bus built in 1993. It went into the Sofia, Bulgaria, fleet in 1996, and is pictured here in 2004. The Chavdar factory in Botevgrad, Bulgaria, a coachbuilder since the late 1920s, built the body for this trolley bus. The Sofia Public Transport Company Elektrotransport AD operates the Sofia trolley bus system. It is one of 15 trolley bus systems in Bulgaria.

# Russia, Belarus, and Ukraine

## *Russia*

The first trolley bus system in Russia opened in Moscow in 1933. It wasn't until after the massive industrialization and electrification following World War II that a steadily increasing number of towns and cities throughout Russia developed trolley bus systems. The trolley bus was seen as modern and progressive.

More trolley bus systems have been built and remain open in Russia than in any other country in the world, and it possesses the world's two largest systems, Moscow and St. Petersburg. Both of these systems have been operating for more than 75 years, and each has had more than 1,000 trolley buses. There are many cities in Russia with well over 100 vehicles.

Trolley bus manufacturing in Russia began early and very few trolley buses have been imported into Russia. In a few cities higher capacity and productivity has been achieved by the use of coupled-set and articulated trolley buses. Three-axle articulated trolley buses didn't begin operating in Russia until quite late, although there were a few four-axle articulateds in Moscow in the 1950s and 1960s. A number of systems operate freight or service vehicles using dual-mode gas/electric vans and trucks.

The Russian-based Uritsky Company, which now operates under the name Trolza, is famous for its ZIU trolley buses. It is probably the world's largest producer of trolley buses, building more than 50,000 vehicles since 1952, most of which have gone to Russian systems, although some have been exported. Other companies in Russia have also been active in trolley bus manufacturing.

Nizhni Novgorod, Russia, celebrated 50 years of trolley bus service in 1997. At the celebration was this restored Model MTB 82 trolley bus, built 50 or more years ago. This model served in great numbers in Russian cities for many years. The MTB 82 was very prevalent in Moscow, but because Nizhni Novgorod (earlier known as Gorky) built some at a former military factory it is reported several MTB 82 trolley buses operated in Nizhni Novgorod. There are approximately 250 trolley buses in Nizhni Novgorod presently. Nizhegorodelektro Trans is the operator of trolley buses in the city.

Saint Petersburg, Russia, established trolley bus service much earlier than most cities in Russia. The first trolley buses were operated in 1936. The system reached a strength of more than 1,000 trolley buses in 1984 and continues to have a large fleet today. Pictured here is one of the Uritsky Model ZIU 9 trolley buses that were acquired in the 1970s. Along with the Model ZIU 10, these two models have been the only types of trolley buses in Saint Petersburg in recent years. Newer trolley buses are entering the Saint Petersburg fleet, including 40 PTZ 5283 trolley buses and 25 Trolza 6245 trolley buses. *O. Iskov*

Rostov-on-Donu, Russia, is one of the almost 100 trolley bus systems operating in Russia. The Tramvaino Trolleibusnoe Upravienic in Rostov-on-Donu operates about 200 trolley buses, most of which are Uritsky ZIU-9 models. One of these trolley buses is pictured. It was built in the early 1990s. The system began in 1936 and was the second Russian trolley bus system after Moscow. While under German occupation from 1941-1945, the system did not operate. In addition to the Russian-built trolley buses, Rostov-on-Donu has eight Den Oudsten trolley buses once operated in Arnhem, Netherlands. *O. Iskov*

The Siberian city of Irkutsk began operating trolley buses in 1970, and the system continues. Pictured in 1975 is one of a number of Uritsky ZIU-9 trolley buses that formed the basic fleet. This trolley bus was delivered in 1973. The present fleet also includes some Uritsky ZIU-10 trolley buses. Irkutsk, with over a half million inhabitants, is one of the larger cities in Siberia. *Bo Lofgren*

The trolley bus system in St. Petersburg, Russia, continues to be one of the largest systems in Europe with approximately 700 vehicles, down from a peak of more than 1,000 trolley buses in the fleet a few years ago. The St. Petersburg system began in 1936. Pictured is a Uritsky Model ZIU-10 trolley bus built in 1990, one of the 27 similar trolley buses delivered in 1990-1991. Gorelectrotrans is the operator of the St. Petersburg trolley bus system. *O. Iskov*

The Nizhegorodelektro Trans is the trolley bus operation in Nizhni Novgorod, Russia. It has been operating trolley buses since 1947 and has a present fleet of about 250 trolley buses. It has three distinct trolley bus operating systems with one on the south side of the Oka River isolated from the other two. One of the system's Uritsky ZIU-9 trolley buses is pictured. These trolley buses are the basic vehicles in the system. Nizhni Novgorod, which is also on the Volga River, has a population of approximately 1.3 million and is the fifth largest city in Russia. *O. Iskov*

## Belarus

One of the largest trolley bus systems in Belarus is in Minsk, its capital. There are reported to be more than 1,000 trolley buses. Most of them have been built in Ukraine, based on the Russian ZIU-682 design. Six other Belarus cities have trolley buses, with three of them operating well over 100 trolley buses.

Brest, Belarus, on the Polish border and actually a Polish city at one time, didn't begin a trolley bus system until 1981. It is the smallest of the seven cities with trolley bus operations in Belarus. The Brest fleet operates approximately 50 vehicles. In contrast, Minsk, the Belarus capital, has more than 1,000 trolley buses. Pictured is a Russian-built ZIU-682 trolley bus on Masherava Avenue in Brest. *Loring M. Lawrence*

## Ukraine

In Ukraine the trolley bus systems are reportedly well run and highly profitable. Kyiv (Kiev) has the country's largest system with more than 600 trolley buses. Kharkov is a close second with more than 500 trolley buses. There are nine other Ukrainian cities each with more than 200 trolley buses in service.

The most remarkable route in Ukraine, and the longest in the world, links a rail head and airport at Simferopol with Yalta, the popular coastal resort, a distance of some 90 km across a high mountain range.

New models of trolley buses, both two-axle and articulated, have appeared recently. A company carrying the name Kiev has been an important trolley bus manufacturer in Ukraine since 1958. It has built some 5,000 trolley buses.

Kyiv (Kiev), the capital of Ukraine, was the first city to establish a trolley bus system in that country. The system began in 1936 with seven trolley buses. It is operated today by the Kyivelektrotrans with 657 trolley buses. In the 1980s there were more than 1,000 trolley buses in Kyiv. One of the newest is this low-floor Model 103T vehicle built by MAZ in Minsk, Belarus, which was delivered in 2005. *Doug Jack*

Pictured is one of the Skoda 346 Model 14 Tr trolley buses that is operated by the Kyivelektrotrans in Kyiv (Kiev), Ukraine. Kyiv has been a good customer for Skoda trolley buses since 1960 when 22 Model 8 Tr trolley buses were acquired. In 1962 Skoda Model 9 Tr trolley buses were added to the fleet. A total of 1,215 Model 9 Tr trolley buses saw service in Kyiv. *Doug Jack*

The trolley bus system operated by Kyivelektrotrans in Kyiv (Kiev), Ukraine, took delivery of 260 DAC Model 217E articulated trolley buses from Autobuzul in Bucharest, Romania, between 1981 and 1990. It has been reported that these trolley buses were fitted with new motors between 1993 and 1995 in the Kyivelektrotrans shops. During 1988 and 1990 the Kyiv system peaked and there were more than 500 million passengers in each of those years. During that time there were 1,000 trolley buses in Kyiv, but downsizing has occurred, reducing the fleet to approximately 650 vehicles. *O. Iskov*

Odesgorelektrans operates the trolley bus system in Odesa (Odessa), Ukraine. The Odesa system began in 1945. It was the third system that was established in Ukraine, which at that time was a part of the Soviet Union. The Odesa trolley bus system is quite large with approximately 270 vehicles. Pictured is one of the Model YuMZ-T1 Yuzmash trolley buses operating on Primorska Boulevard. It and 26 other trolley buses built by Yuzmash in 1993 are in the Odesa fleet. *O. Iskov*

Pictured is a Model YuMZ-T2 trolley bus operating in Sevastopol, Ukraine. It was built in 1994 at the Yuzmash factory in Dnepropatrovsk, Ukraine, which began building trolley buses in 1993. The Sevastopol system began in 1950 and continues to operate today. It is one of the several large trolley bus systems in Ukraine with more than 200 vehicles. Also in the picture is a Uritsky Model ZIU-9 trolley bus built in Russia about 1990. A large fleet of ZIU trolley buses, including Model TTB 82d trolley buses from the 1950s, operated in Sevastopol. *O. Iskov*

Kyiv (Kiev) is one of the 48 cities in Ukraine that operates trolley buses. The system began in 1935. Kyiv has operated 100 Skoda Model 14 Tr trolley buses, one of which is pictured here in 1997, in addition to sizable fleets of Skoda Model 15 Tr articulated trolley buses. There are a total of approximately 650 trolley buses operating in Kyiv at the present time. Newer trolley buses built in the Ukraine are now being acquired. *O. Iskov*

A three-door Uritsky Model ZIU-9 trolley bus built about 1990 is seen at the Odesa (Odessa), Ukraine, trolley bus and bus terminal Dzershinskogo pl in July 1997. Odesa has had a large fleet of ZIU-9 trolley buses, but in recent years a number of Ukraine-built Yuzmash Model YuMZ articulated and standard trolley buses have been added. The Odesa trolley bus system is operated by Odesgorelektrans. *O. Iskov*

# Australia & New Zealand

## Australia

Urban transport operators in Australia were strongly influenced by Britain, although the first trolley bus was a conversion from a locally built motor bus. All Australian trolley buses used British-built chassis, although the majority were single-deck models.

Perth had the first and the last system, beginning in 1933 and continuing until 1969. It was a moderate network for the size of the city. The Adelaide trolley bus system was similar. Sydney's trolley bus system consisted of one route east of the central area and a two-branch line in the far southeastern suburbs. Brisbane also had trolley buses from 1951 to 1969.

It is interesting to note that the second-largest city in Australia, Melbourne, never operated trolley buses.

In the two Tasmanian cities of Hobart and Launceston, trolley buses formed the most important part of the basic system of transportation and were enthusiastically supported.

The Metropolitan Passenger Transport Trust of Perth, Australia, operated a trolley bus system between 1933 and 1968. Perth was the last of six Australian cities to discontinue trolley buses. The first four Perth trolley buses were Model TTB1 Leylands from England, delivered in 1933. An interesting feature was that the trolley poles were mounted above one another. Perth had 90 trolley buses, 40 built by Leyland and 50 by the British firm Sunbeam Trolleybus Company, Ltd. *John Banks Collection*

One trolley bus was operated in Adelaide, Australia, from 1932 through 1934. In 1937 the Adelaide Municipal Tramways Trust began replacing motor bus and tram routes with trolley buses. The Model MF 2B trolley bus pictured had a chassis built by the British firm Sunbeam and a body by the Australian body building company J. A. Lawton and Sons. There were 30 of this type of trolley bus in the Adelaide fleet. They were delivered in 1952-1953.

Hobart (Australia) Municipal Tramways began trolley bus operations in Hobart, in the Australian state of Tasmania, in 1935. The service continued until 1968. Pictured is a Leyland Model TB5, one of the 20 acquired in 1942. The chassis of this trolley bus was among 70 destined for Canton, China, but because of the Japanese occupation of China, these trolley bus chassis were diverted to several transit systems, including Adelaide. Bodies for these diverted trolley buses were constructed over four-and-a-half years in the Hobart shops. *Ian Cooper*

Pictured is a 1950 BUT ETB1 trolley bus, one of 36 acquired by the Hobart (Australia) Municipal Tramways beginning in 1950. The bodies of these trolley buses were assembled and finished by City Body Works with lightweight pressed steel sections supplied by Commonwealth Engineering. *Ian Cooper*

Two 1951 BUT Model ETB1 trolley buses in Launceston, Tasmania, Australia, are pictured in March 1968, four months prior to the end of trolley bus service in Launceston. The trolley bus depot is the large building in the background. Launceston Municipal Tramways was the original operator of Launceston trolley buses. In 1955 the Tasmanian state assumed the trolley bus operations in both Hobart and Launceston. *Ian Cooper*

Launceston, Tasmania, Australia, began a trolley bus system in 1951. The system was the only regional city of the six Australian cities that operated trolley buses. Pictured is one of the 30 BUT ETB1 trolley buses that Launceston Municipal Tramways put into service in 1957 to replace the city's trams. They had bodies by J. A. Lawton and Sons of Adelaide. *Ian Cooper*

## New Zealand

Trolley bus systems in New Zealand were developed very early. Wellington had its first system in 1924 and Christchurch in 1931. However, the early Wellington system was discontinued in 1932. Trolley buses were reinstated in Wellington in 1949 and service continues today.

Until deliveries of Volvo trolley buses to Wellington in the 1980s, all trolley buses used British-built chassis, and many vehicles had British-built or British-designed bodies. Manufacturers in Australia completed many of the trolley bus bodies, and the operators themselves also built many of the trolley bus bodies.

The systems in Auckland and Dunedin lasted until the early 1980s. New Plymouth, the smallest of the cities in New Zealand to have a trolley bus system, had only one route and four vehicles.

In 1950 Dunedin (New Zealand) Corporation Transport Department began trolley bus service with British BUT RETB1 trolley buses. A total of 79 similar vehicles were added to the Dunedin fleet before 1962. A phasing out of the trolley bus service began in the late 1960s, and service came to an end in 1982. One of the BUT trolley buses is pictured in downtown Dunedin in 1976. New Zealand Motor Bodies built the bodies for Dunedin trolley buses 1 to 55, and the Corporation built the bodies for 56 to 79.

In 1957 this BUT RETB 1-2 trolley bus was imported by the Auckland (New Zealand) Transport Board. It had a complete chassis and body by Park Royal in England and a special red waistband. This was one of 15 Queen Street shuttle trolley buses in Auckland. It was photographed on Christmas Day in 1961 with "Seasons Greetings" signs displayed on the vehicle. Most of the Auckland trolley buses were BUT RETB 1-2s with CKD bodies assembled in the Auckland Transport shops. *Ian Cooper*

Auckland (New Zealand) Transport Board began operating trolley buses in 1938. The service continued until 1980. Pictured is one of the 74 BUT RET1 trolley buses. The chassis came to Auckland in 1955. The Saunders Roe company in England supplied the CKD bodies that were assembled in the Auckland Transport Board shops. *Ian Cooper*

Wellington (New Zealand) City Transport began trolley bus operations in 1949 and it continues today. The Wellington service operated 109 BUT RETB1 trolley buses, delivered between 1951 and 1964. They had bodies by Commonwealth Engineering of Sydney, Australia. The bodies were supplied by CKD and assembled in the Wellington City Council's workshops. A one-vehicle trolley bus service operated in Wellington from 1924 to 1932. *Ian Cooper*

The Wellington (New Zealand) City Corporation Transport Department began a trolley bus system in 1949, although an earlier one-vehicle line operated in Wellington for eight years beginning in 1924. In 1964 Scammel Lorries in Britain delivered 37 trolley buses of the BUT RETB1 design to Wellington. They had bodies built by Metropolitan-Cammel-Weymann, Ltd., also in Britain, and New Zealand Motor Bodies. One of these trolley buses is pictured in downtown Wellington in 1976, one year before it was withdrawn from service.

Wellington is one of five cities that had trolley bus systems in New Zealand. Trolley bus service in Wellington began in 1949, and it is the only New Zealand trolley bus system that continues today. An earlier trolley bus system in Wellington began in 1924 but ended eight years later. The trolley bus pictured is a Volvo Model B58 with a body by the New Zealand firm Hawke Motor Bodies. Hawke supplied 33 of this type of trolley bus to Wellington between 1981 and 1983.

In 1983, 20 Volvo B10M trolley buses went into service in Wellington, New Zealand. They had bodies by New Zealand Motor Bodies with Hess (Switzerland) design. These 20 trolley buses were originally to go to Auckland, but that system closed three years earlier. When these trolley buses were delivered, Wellington was the only one of five New Zealand cities to continue operating trolley buses. Although there have been concerns that the Wellington trolley bus system would close, it continues today.

The British Stagecoach Group became the operator of the transit system in Wellington, New Zealand, in 1992. The system is known as Stagecoach Wellington. When Stagecoach acquired the system, 60 trolley buses were included. At that time the Wellington fleet of trolley buses was nearing replacement age. In 2003, Designline Coachbuilders of Ashburton, New Zealand, built this prototype trolley bus, which has been undergoing tests in Wellington. If successful, an order for a number of similar trolley buses is expected. However, the Stagecoach Group is selling its New Zealand holdings; therefore, the status of the new trolley bus situation for Wellington is not known. *Loring M. Lawrence*

# East Asia

## *China*

China has had 28 trolley bus systems and some cities have very large fleets of 200 or more vehicles.

Most interesting is the trolley bus system in Shanghai, China's largest city. It began in 1914 and continues today, and is the oldest continuously operated trolley bus system in the world. It has also been one of the world's largest systems, with nearly 1,000 trolley buses at one time.

The Shanghai trolley bus system has been changing in recent years. In the latter part of the 20th Century articulated trolley buses were most common on all routes, but in the 21st Century, new, smaller standard trolley buses have been introduced. These are of very modern design, and quite often air-conditioned. Volvo Buses of Sweden has a joint venture with a Shanghai builder and is building many of the new trolley buses.

Beijing, China's capital and second largest city, has the second-largest trolley bus fleet in the country. There has been an emphasis on modernization of the system in preparation for the 2008 Olympic Games scheduled for Beijing. The trolley bus modernization is similar to the situation that took place in Athens, Greece, prior to the 2004 Olympic Games.

Other than Shanghai, no other trolley bus system in China was established prior to 1950. Between 1950 and 1980, 27 systems were launched, but in recent years, eight of these systems have closed, including a very large trolley bus system in Shenyang (Mukden). It had its beginning in 1951 and had more than 500 vehicles. The system closed in 1999. Even the Shanghai system is experiencing discontinuance of some of its trolley bus routes.

In recent years there has been talk about introducing trolley buses to crowded Hong Kong, which was returned to China after being a modern British colonial city for more than 100 years. An experimental double-deck trolley bus has been undergoing tests on a special track in Hong Kong, but there has been no information about a new trolley bus system being established in the near future.

Trolley bus manufacturing has been very active throughout the last 50 to 60 years, mainly to supply local needs. There have been a few examples of trolley bus exports from China to Nepal, Chile, and Argentina. This has taken place in very recent years.

Most trolley buses operating in China have been built at the transportation systems' workshops. The basic design of the vehicles has been virtually the same in all the trolley bus cities.

Little is known about trolley bus history in China because of the isolation of the country for many years and the difficulty of communicating, even in the modern era. No doubt some students of trolley bus history will find the opportunity to uncover very interesting information about the trolley bus history of China in the not-to-distant future.

Dalian in Northern China is one of the cities in China with a population of more than one million with a sizable trolley bus system. There are more than 200 trolley buses operating in the area. One of the articulated Model DL-72C Dalian-built trolley buses is pictured. *Danny Chan*

Guangzhou, China, has a large trolley bus system that was established in 1960 and continues to operate today. Pictured is one of the new trolley buses built by the Shanghai Automotive Industry Corporation. Most of the new trolley buses operating in Guangzhou are air-conditioned. The trolley buses are also equipped with batteries for off-wire operation. *Danny Chan*

In 2000 articulated trolley buses were being phased out in Shanghai, China, and being replaced by smaller trolley buses. The articulated trolley buses operated with a driver and a ticket collector. The smaller vehicles maneuver easier among heavy bicycle traffic. Pictured is one of the smaller trolley buses in downtown Shanghai. The Shanghai Bashi Trolley Bus Co., Ltd. became the name of the major trolley bus services in Shanghai, as the result of the merger of three companies in 2002. *Danny Chan*

Shanghai Automotive Industry Corporation has been building modern trolley buses for a number of systems in China, including many for Shanghai. A new trolley bus is pictured here. The trolley buses in Shanghai are usually 11.5 or 10 meters long and are said to be more efficient on Shanghai's streets. Note the advertising on the trolley bus. It is an indication of changes taking place in 21st Century China. *Danny Chan*

There have been 31 cities in China with trolley bus systems and all but seven continue today. Shanghai's trolley bus system has been operating the longest, just over 90 years. Recently Shanghai had 22 trolley bus routes and a peak of more than 900 vehicles. Early types of trolley buses have been like the one pictured here in 1996. Most trolley buses of this type were built in the operators' shops and little other information is available. *Danny Chan*

Trolley bus service in the Chinese capital city of Beijing began in 1957 and continues with a sizable fleet. One of the newest trolley buses of the Beijing Public Transport is shown in the center of the capital. The trolley bus fleet is being upgraded in preparation for the 2008 Olympic Games, which will be hosted by Beijing. Latest information indicates that there are 500 trolley buses in Beijing. *Danny Chan*

## Japan

Six large Japanese cities had trolley bus systems in the past, with the largest ones in Osaka and Tokyo. All of these systems were discontinued prior to 1970.

An unusual system began in 1964, connecting a tourist resort and a dam. It was originally used by construction vehicles working on the dam project. Most of the route lies underground in a single-track tunnel. A separate company runs a similar system that began in 1996 in a neighboring tunnel.

This trolley bus is a Type 200 that went into service for the Tokyo Municipal Transportation Bureau (TMTB) in 1954. There were 39 of this type of trolley bus, 25 of which were built in 1954 and 14 that were built in 1956. The chassis builder was Hino and the body builder was Fuji Heavy Industries. All 39 went into TMTB service. The first 35 of these trolley buses received new bodies in 1962-1963. Tokyo's trolley bus system ended in 1968.

Tokyo, Japan, was one of the seven Japanese cities that operated trolley buses. The Tokyo Municipal Transportation Bureau (TMTB) began in 1952. The trolley bus pictured is one of 20 that came to the TMTB in 1957-1958. These trolley buses, known as Type 50s, had Hino chassis, Fuji Heavy Industries bodies, and Toshiba motors. They were originally built for Tientsin, China, but because of export restrictions they remained in Japan and were acquired by TMTB, where they received new bodies. The picture shows the trolley buses with the original bodies.

The Yokohama (Japan) Municipal Transportation Bureau had a small trolley bus service between 1959 and 1972. Pictured is a Mitsubishi TB14 trolley bus with a Tokyo Sharyo body. It and 14 others went into service in Yokohama between 1959 and 1962. *Yukio Wada*

Pictured is a 1962 Mitsubishi TB14 trolley bus, one of five with Fuji Heavy Industries bodies in service by the Yokohama (Japan) Municipal Transportation Bureau in 1963. Seven cities in Japan operated trolley buses over the years, but there are no longer trolley buses in any major Japanese city. Yokohama was the last of the major Japanese cities to discontinue trolley buses. *Yukio Wada*

One of two trolley bus operations that continue in Japan is at the Kurobe Dam in the Japanese Alps, primarily for transportation of sightseers. Pictured in the system's tunnel is one of the 15 Type 300 trolley buses introduced in 1993. The chassis is by Mitsubishi. The Taleyama Kurobe Kanko (TKK) operates the trolley bus service. *Yukio Wada*

## Malaysia

The trolley bus system of Georgetown Municipal Transport, Penang, Malaysia (formerly Malaya), began very early, operating from 1924 to 1961. It operated the only double-deck trolley buses on the Asian mainland, five secondhand vehicles from London. The system took delivery of 25 modern trolley buses from 1953 to 1958.

## North Korea

Little is known about the trolley bus system in the Democratic People's Republic of Korea (North Korea). The capital, Pyongyang, has a very large system with more than 400 two-axle and articulated trolley buses.

## Philippines

The Philippines had two different trolley bus systems for a brief time, both of them in Manila, the capital. The first operated from 1924 to 1928 with two Atlas/General Electric vehicles running on solid tires on a route inside the old city walls. The second used eight Twin Coach trolley buses with central doorways. After 1939 they was no trolley bus activity in the Philippines.

## Singapore

The island nation of Singapore was one of the earliest to completely convert from trams to trolley buses and was, for a time, the world's largest trolley bus system. The first vehicles had open-air fronts and solid tires, a unique design suited to the tropical climate. World War II took a heavy toll on the fleet and a new, but smaller, fleet was supplied from Britain. The service was discontinued in 1962.

# Central & South Asia

## Armenia, Azerbaijan, Georgia, Kazakhstan, Turkmenistan, Uzbekistan, Tadzhikistan and Kyrghystan

These Central Asian countries have approximately 50 active trolley bus operations. Many cities have trolley bus systems, including some very small ones with small fleets. There are also very large trolley bus fleets, particularly in Tbilisi, Georgia, which have more than 100 vehicles, and Tashkent, Uzbekistan, with more than 300 trolley buses. Several cities have more than 200 trolley buses, most of which have been built in Russia. Skoda has delivered a number of trolley buses to cities in these countries.

## Afghanistan

In Kabul, the capital of Afghanistan, a network of three routes using Skoda trolley buses was created after the country came under communist control in the late 1970s. The present trolley bus situation is unknown.

## India

Although India has had trolley bus systems in the past, the trolley bus never developed into a major form of permanent transport. There have been some indications that the reintroduction of trolley buses is being contemplated to answer concerns about congestion and pollution.

## Iran

Iran became one of the newest trolley bus operating countries in the world in 1992 when a single route began in the capital, Tehran, with Skoda articulated trolley buses. Nearly the whole route is located in a reserved space in the middle of the main roads, to keep the trolley buses separate from other vehicles in the chaotic traffic conditions.

Samarkand, Uzbekistan, is the second largest city in the country. It was also the second Uzbekistan city to begin operating trolley buses. That was in 1957, and the city continues to operate trolley buses. A Uritsky ZIU-9 trolley bus is pictured in 1975 in operation on one of five routes. There are nine trolley bus systems in Uzbekistan. The largest is in Toshkent, the capital and largest city. *Bo Lofgren*

## Nepal

The abundance of hydroelectric power coming from the Himalayas was the basis for the system that opened in Kathmandu, the capital of Nepal, in 1975. Backed by Chinese finance, vehicle supply, and construction, the Kathmandu system had only Chinese-built trolley buses. They were the only Chinese vehicles to have been exported until the sale of Chinese vehicles to Chile in 1991. The Kathmandu trolley bus system has had difficulties in recent years with intermittent closures, but has managed to continue operations.

## Sri Lanka

The island of Sri Lanka, formerly Ceylon, operated trolley buses on a short-lived trolley bus system in the city of Colombo from 1953 to 1964. Most of the fleet of more than 60 vehicles consisted of double-deck trolley buses from Britain.

The Nepal Transport Corporation began a 22-vehicle trolley bus system for the Nepalese capital city, Kathmandu, in 1975. The 22 trolley buses were built in Shanghai, China, and carried model number SK 541. One is pictured here. They operate using the left-hand rule of the road. The system has had slowdowns and curtailments, but further financial assistance keeps it running until the next challenge. *Photographer unknown, Cliff Scholes collection*

The Colombo Municipal Passenger Transport Department in Colombo, Ceylon (now Sri Lanka), operated trolley buses for 11 years, beginning in 1953. The first Colombo trolley buses were 20 BUT 9611 double-deck vehicles with Weymann bodies. Colombo began the system in 1953 with 35 of these trolley buses. *John Banks Collection*

## Turkey

Trolley buses have not played a major role in urban transport in Turkey, but at one time three systems, located in Istanbul, Ankara, and Izmir, operated some 220 trolley buses. New U.S.-built ACF-Brill trolley buses operated in Ankara. MAN and Italian-built trolley buses operated in Ankara and Izmir. Istanbul also operated Italian-built trolley buses. The trolley bus system in Izmir lasted until 1992. Ankara and Istanbul closed their systems in 1980.

Electricity Gas and Omnibus (EGO), the transportation system in Ankara, Turkey, began trolley bus service in 1946 with 10 ACF-Brill TC44 trolley buses with General Electric motors. They were imported from the United States. These Ankara trolley buses were the only units built by ACF-Brill that were sold new overseas. This ACF-Brill trolley bus is pictured in service in 1975, almost 30 years after the vehicle was acquired. The Ankara trolley bus system closed in 1986. MAN/Kassbohrer from Germany and Alfa Romeo/Ansaldo from Italy built other trolley buses in Ankara. *Wilhelm Pflug*

Izmir, Turkey, once known as Smyrna, a port city on the Aegean coast, was one of three Turkish cities that operated trolley buses. The service in Izmir began in 1954 by the Elektrik Su Havagazi Otobus Troleybus (ESHOT). Pictured is one of 18 German Bussing Model U110 trolley buses with Turkish bodywork acquired in 1968. There were six trolley buses operated by ESHOT and about 100 trolley buses in the fleet. By comparison there were 600 motor buses. The use of trolley buses in Izmir ended in 1992. It was the last of the cities in Turkey to discontinue trolley bus service. *Bo Lofgren*

Istanbul, Turkey, had trolley buses in service for 22 years. The first and only trolley buses to operate in the system were 100 Fiat-Alfa Romeo trolley buses from Italy, which were delivered in 1962-1963. They had electrical equipment by the Italian firm Ansaldo. The Istanbul transportation system was operated by Istanbul Elektrik Tramvay ve Tunel.

Izmir, Turkey, began operating trolley buses in 1954. This MAN trolley bus and 17 others were the first to be operated by the Elektrik Su Havagazi Otobus Troleybus company. The system in Izmir closed in 1992. At one time there were 90 vehicles in its fleet, some of which had been in service since 1957. No trolley buses are currently being operated in Turkey. *Wilhelm Pflug*

# Africa

## Algeria

The capital, El Djesair (Alger), had two separate systems that joined in 1959. The city had extremely steep and tortuous routes, beyond the physical capability of the tram system. In many ways an ideal form of transport for the environment, the trolley bus system fell into decline after the country achieved independence and developed its oil resources. Three other cities operated trolley bus routes in Algeria.

## Egypt

El Qahira (Cairo), the capital of Egypt, had a large but poorly maintained tram system, and its trolley buses were equally neglected, at least in later years. A compact and intensive network was developed on the west bank of the Nile River that also crossed the river. The system was very large with more than 100 trolley buses.

El Qahira (Cairo), Egypt, was one of several North African cities that operated trolley buses in the past. The Cairo trolley buses were first introduced in 1950. The network grew considerably when tram routes on the west bank of the Nile River were closed in 1959-1960. In 1973 there were 160 trolley buses operating in Cairo, 114 of which were needed during peak service. The picture shows one of the 120 Turbocar T45 trolley buses that were delivered around 1960. The chassis was by the Italian Alfa Romeo firm, the bodywork by Casara, and electric equipment was from CGE. Trolley bus service ended in Cairo in 1987.

Morocco, in northwestern Africa, once had two trolley bus systems, one in Tetuan and the other, a much larger one, operated by the La Regie Autonome de Transports en Commune de Casablanca. The Casablanca trolley bus pictured, a Vetra, entered service in the late 1950s. It was part of a 40-trolley bus purchase. To provide maximum ventilation in Morocco's hot climate, the side windows could completely slide down within the body sides. Trolley bus service began in Casablanca in 1932 and continued until closure 50 years later.
*Loring M. Lawrence*

Johannesburg (South Africa) Transport Department began operating trolley buses in 1936. The next year several AEC trolley buses with Metropolitan-Cammel-Weymann bodies were imported from England. These were double-deck trolley buses with two axles. Each had seating for 60 passengers and space for 12 standing passengers. The Johannesburg trolley bus system survived for 50 years until 1986.

## Morocco

In Casablanca the trolley bus system reflected the influence of France, the whole fleet being supplied by Vetra. The only other trolley bus system was in Titwan.

## South Africa

The most important center of trolley bus operations on the African continent was in South Africa, with three very early systems and four substantial operations in the modern era.

Systems in Bloemfontein, Boksburg, and Germiston operated trolley buses as early as 1914, but ended prior to 1940. In the mid-1930s, four of the larger cities of South Africa began converting their tram systems to trolley buses. Cape Town, Durban, and Pretoria had modern trolley bus systems that continued into the 1960s and 1970s. Johannesburg, which began using trolley buses in 1938, operated the largest trolley bus system in South Africa with 165 trolley buses.

After World War II, a large number of double-deck trolley buses were acquired from Britain and used in the larger South African cities. Cape Town also had some single-deck trolley buses. Double-deck trolley buses were the last to be used before trolley bus services ended.

## Tunisia

Tunis, the capital of Tunisia, operated a trolley bus system with French-built Vetras. The system, which began in 1937, did not increase in size and was discontinued in 1970.

There were experiments with trolley buses in South Africa as early as 1914, but those services were short-lived. Then in the mid-1930s, trolley bus service was inaugurated in four of the largest South African cities, including Pretoria. Pictured is one of the 10 Leyland trolley buses that was part of the original fleet delivered to Pretoria in 1938, along with 24 single-deck Leyland trolley buses. The trolley bus service operated by the Pretoria City Council Transport ended in 1972.

In 1958, 50 BUT 9642T three-axle, double-deck trolley buses entered service for the Johannesburg (South Africa) Transport Department. These large trolley buses had seating for 73 passengers and 12 standees were allowed. They had bodies built by Bus Bodies, a South African bus body builder. These trolley buses underwent some rebuilding to convert to one-man operation. The Johannesburg trolley bus system was quite large and had 175 trolley buses in 1963. By 1982, four years before closing, the fleet had been reduced to 66 vehicles.

# Trolley Bus Preservation

There have been many manufacturers and models of trolley buses over the years. Fortunately, many trolley bus historians and enthusiasts have recognized the importance of preserving this significant part of the transportation history of the world.

It is estimated that more than 600 historic trolley buses have been preserved. Some operating systems have kept the historic trolley buses they once operated, either on their own property or by giving them to museums in their area. Trolley bus historic societies, museums, and individuals have acquired other vintage trolley buses. Preserved trolley buses are housed in many locations.

Those operating systems that continue to operate trolley bus services often keep the preserved trolley buses in operating condition. Trolley bus historians and enthusiasts can run these trolley buses on special occasions, such as historic days, or for excursions. When Salzburg, Austria, recently celebrated 65 years of trolley bus service, the festivities included the operation of both old and new trolley buses on the city's existing trolley bus lines. In the United States, the city of Seattle, Washington, often operates special excursions using preserved trolley buses on the city's present trolley bus route system.

There are preserved trolley buses in most countries of the world where trolley buses were important. Some are in museums and some are preserved on the properties of operating systems. Some have special infrastructure that allows the preserved trolley buses

One of the preserved trolley buses in New Zealand is in the Tramway Historical Society museum in Ferrymeade, New Zealand. It was one of the first six trolley buses acquired by the Christchurch (New Zealand) Tramway Board in 1931. It had a chassis built in England by the English Electric Company, Ltd. with a Boon and Company body. The Christchurch trolley bus system closed in 1956. *Loring M. Lawrence*

to be operated on the museum property for visitors. Sometimes vintage city buildings and other settings make the trolley bus operations at the museums very realistic.

For a small country, New Zealand has a remarkable number of preserved trolley buses. These include several in operating condition. One of the most interesting operating museums is The Motor Coach Museum Trust in Foxton, near Wellington. It features preserved trolley buses from systems that operated in Auckland, Dunedin, and New Plymouth, as well as from Wellington, the only trolley bus system still in operation in New Zealand. Seven of the preserved trolley buses of the Foxton museum operate on public streets and roads in the community, which makes the museum very unusual and most interesting. There is also the Ferrymeade Historic Park near Christchurch, which has two restored trolley buses operating on a short route.

In Britain, where preservation of history is important to many, an estimated 150 once-operating trolley buses have been preserved. Most were part of trolley bus systems in British cities and have been saved by the operating systems. They are found in museums, or are owned by trolley bus historical societies or individuals.

The largest British trolley bus museum is the Sandoft Transport Museum near Doncaster. It has 46 trolley buses, many of which have been restored. Some are in operating condition and can be run on the special wired route on the property. Other British trolley buses of the past are on display at the East Anglica Museum at Carlton Colville, which has a wired route for the operation of the trolley buses.

In the United States there are close to 100 preserved trolley buses. Some are in museums, some are owned by individuals, and some have been kept by various present operating systems. The Illinois Railway Museum, which features various transportation vehicles, is able to operate some of its historic trolley buses on its property in Union, Illinois.

Because of the worldwide interest in trolley buses, especially by historians, there have been many books published about trolley bus history. The *World Trolleybus Encyclopaedia* by Alan Murray is especially informative, with pictures and considerable data.

In the United Kingdom there have been countless books written about trolley buses, either about trolley buses operating in individual cities or about trolley buses in general. Informative books on trolley buses have also been published in many other countries operating trolley buses, including Germany, France, Italy, Sweden, and Norway. Other books have featured the history of trolley buses in specific cities, such as Salzburg, Solingen, Lyon, and a number of cities in the Czech Republic.

Many books on trolley bus history were researched in the writing of this book and yielded a great deal of information for the text and the picture captions. A list of all those books is included in the Bibliography.

# Index

# Index of cities

# More Great Titles From
# Iconografix

All Iconografix books are available from direct mail specialty book dealers and bookstores worldwide, or can be ordered from the publisher. For book trade and distribution information or to add your name to our mailing list and receive a **FREE CATALOG** contact:

### Iconografix, Inc.
PO Box 446, Dept BK
Hudson, WI, 54016

Telephone: (715) 381-9755, (800) 289-3504 (USA), Fax: (715) 381-9756
**info@iconografixinc.com**
**www.iconografixinc.com**

# More great books from Iconografix

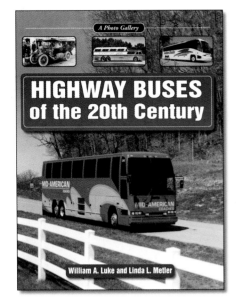

ISBN 1-58388-121-2

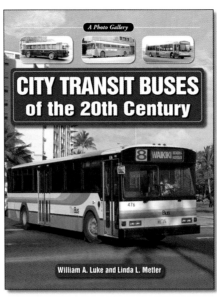

ISBN 1-58388-146-8

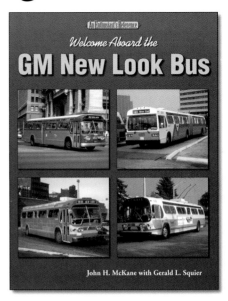

ISBN 1-58388-167-0

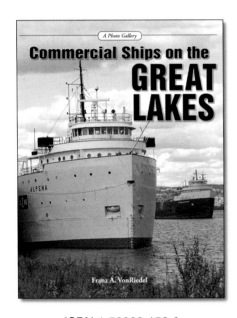

ISBN 1-58388-153-0

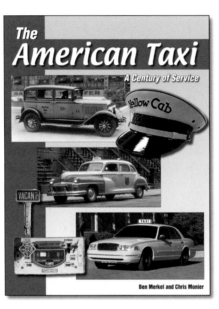

ISBN 1-58388-176-X

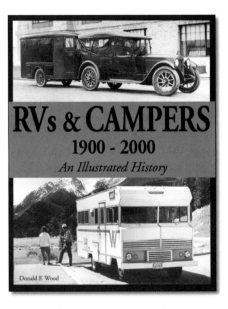

ISBN 1-58388-064-X

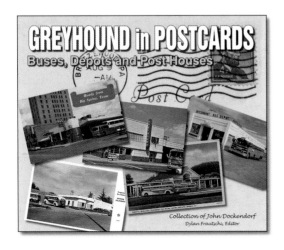

ISBN 1-58388-130-1

## Iconografix, Inc.

P.O. Box 446, Dept BK,
Hudson, WI 54016
**For a free catalog call:** 1-800-289-3504
info@iconografixinc.com
www.iconografixinc.com